The Truth...

What it *really* takes to make it in Network Marketing

Created and written by
Kim Klaver

Max Out Productions
4741 Central Suite 300
Kansas City MO 64112
816.333.6619
visit our web site at: www.maxout.com

ISBN #1-891493-05-1
First Edition

Created and written by Kim Klaver

Design and Editing by Paula English
Illustration by Brian Cano
Inking by Steve Leialoha
Color by House of Color, SF CA

The Cast

Magic Mike
Hot to Trot
Quickscore
Bob Hype
Peanut Gallery
...especially with a little care. This might be a chance for us to help them at a deeper level...
Thera P. & friend & Woo Wu
Zayno Furst
ZOP
Ms. Stud!
Slo Moe
Hope Springs
Accountant
Pukeys

The Show

I The Great Fake Out
It's not what they told you
Plague of the pukeys
Introducing Zayno Furst

II So, where do we get 'em then?
Make 'em come to you
You go first
Letters, calls, ads, decks, streetwalking, bump intos...
Doing it and saying it
The Blitz

III Keeping it together
Doing it in teams
How long will it take?
Goodbye message

IV Just for you
Leading questions
Knock 'em off the fence
You pick

Vendors and Resellers
Index

The Great Fake Out...

Did you hear that? That guy up there said he's making $5500 a month and he's only been in the business for 6 weeks!
Aghh, I know! I can't stand it. I've just GOT to do this, don't choo?
And that woman with 3 kids...wha'd she say she's making? Enough to move into a new house and send her kids to private school?
An' she says she got her energy and health back with those supplements. If I could just get some energy, I could do a business like this and take care of my family.

Ah'm a trucker an' ah've only been doin' this for 6 days. Already ah got 9 people in wi' me. Ah'm gonna be quittin' my job soon!
I've sold 17 customers already, and I haven't even been home for Spring break yet! This is easier than getting a marketing degree... makes $$ faster, too!
Well, folks, do you want to make a change or stay the way you are???? These folks did it! What about you? Think you're up to it? Whaddaya say? Think you're as good as they are?

Yeah! I think I can do this...and I want a new car. If they can do it, I can too.
Piece of cake! We need a quick buck! We'll be rich in a few weeks! Nothing to it! We've hit the jackpot...wowowow! Can't wait! We're gonna be RICH RICH RICH!!

Well, what'll it be? Do you wanna make a change or stay the way you are???
EXIT
APPLICATIONS

Yeah, I wanna do this. I like the product and I think other people will, too. So whadda I hafta do to get rich with this?
Easy! All ya hafta do is make a list of all your friends, family and neighbors and just EVERYBODY in the world that you know! Got a holiday card list? Who do ya know? Who do ya know?
And who do THEY know? And who do THEY know???
Ok, then what??
Hey!! Just tell 'em about all the money they can make and how the stuff gives you sex appeal and yer youth back. An' don't everybody you know need money? Hit 'em ALL up! This is it! They can get rich rich rich!! This is the greatest deal in the history of the world! Gotta go...call me later and tell me how many people you signed up!
BOB HYPE
Awwrighhhhht! Let's go get rich and save everybody we know!
SLAM

Hi, Jerry? Hey listen...I've got a way to get rich. This is your chance to get out of that hole you live in... Wanna get rich with me?
Whaddaya mean, what am I smoking? Lemme tell you all about it...it's the greatest deal in the history of the world.
Can you believe that? I thought he was my friend!
Uncle Donald needs money--and he's not very healthy either. He's always complaining. He'll LOVE this...
ACK

Uncle Donald? Hi! It's Hot to Trot and I'm calling you because I've started my own business...and I...
Who's this? HOT! We've been worrying about you. Where have you been? Why haven't you called? MARTHA! Hot's on the phone...yes!
...you know how you're always complaining about money, well, I have a way to get lots of it. Ye-yess...my own business and I saw lots of people making big money doing it. And it's a wonderful product.
Your own business? They took you for a sucker, that's for sure. Whadya go to school for all those years? Can'tcha get a real job?
You can't make any money with them things! And some them are even illegal! What's wrong with you???
Boy, a lot of good you are when I need you. This isn't gonna be as easy as we thought. There must be a trick to it.
Yeah yeah— there's a trick to it!!

Hey Joe--hey listen...If I could show you a way to get healthy and make big money at the same time, and it could fit into your schedule, would you wanna check it out?
Uhhh... I don't know. Is it one of those things? Would I have to spend my own money? And anyway, how do I know it's not a scam?
Do you think I'd be doing it if it were?
How would you know, anyway? My brother knows someone who once lost big money in one of those deals, over $93, I don't think-
There goes the quick money--rats!

I used to be an accountant. I've just quit my job--I make more in a month now than I did in 6 months in my old job.

It wasn't easy at first...some people laughed. But I believed in this business and in myself. And now I'm laughing--all the way to the bank!
D'ya hear that? I wanna laugh all the way to the bank! That'll show 'em!
Go baby!! Laugh all the way to the bank!
Well ladies and gents--as you just heard, ANYONE can do this. It takes persistence, belief in yourself and the business, and NEVER give up.
Easy for him to say- -he's already rich.
Yeah, cliches! Cliches everywhere!
Our company's been around for years! Thousands of distributors sell our product line; everybody has the same comp plan... so what makes one person more successful than another? Any idea? Mmmm??
LOSER DUST
No!
Boo!! That's not all there is!!!

Uhh...I was wondering if you could tell me how you're doing this. I'm not having much success yet.
What do you mean, what deal is it? The greatest one in the history of the world! That's what you said. What other deal? Oh. You're out of this one? Another greatest deal in the world?!
Listen, I can't even do the one I've got. No thanks. Anyway, I like this product.
Maybe I'll just use the stuff and forget the business... Nah, I don't think it's for me. Sorry. Bye!

R-R-ING

Hey, is this Hot t'Trot? I'm calling to congratulate you...
...for joining our business. I saw your name on my geneology report and wanted to see if there was anything I could do for you.
Well, uhhh, I dunno...I don't think I can do this.
...I have 21,000 people in my business now and make pretty obscene income, but I always like to introduce myself to new people in my business. How's the product working for you?

Obscene income?
Gosh- yeah, the product works great. I don't know if I can do the business though. I can't get anyone to even listen to me...and the people I know, well, uh, they were, uhhh
Pukey, huh? Ugh! I hate when that happens.
She KNO-O-WS!!!!
Y'know, before I started making big money, they used to do the same thing to me.
They did???
Anyway, just when I was ready to give up on the idea, I heard somebody tell how to do it the real way. That's when I started making the big bucks.
Oh yeah? What 'real way'? Where's that person? Are they around? How do I talk to them?

Well, there's a special affair near you--at the University of Hollywood.
Go. Then decide if you can do the business or not. 'zat sound reasonable?
Uh, yeah, ok. So when and where and what...?
YESSS!!!!
EO
SKOOL 4 DUMMIES

University of Hollywood
LIVE!!! Ms. Stud!
Wonder who's playing there...the Stones?
Think they're still around?
LOOK!!!
And you thought you were the only ones!!! Heh heh heh!!

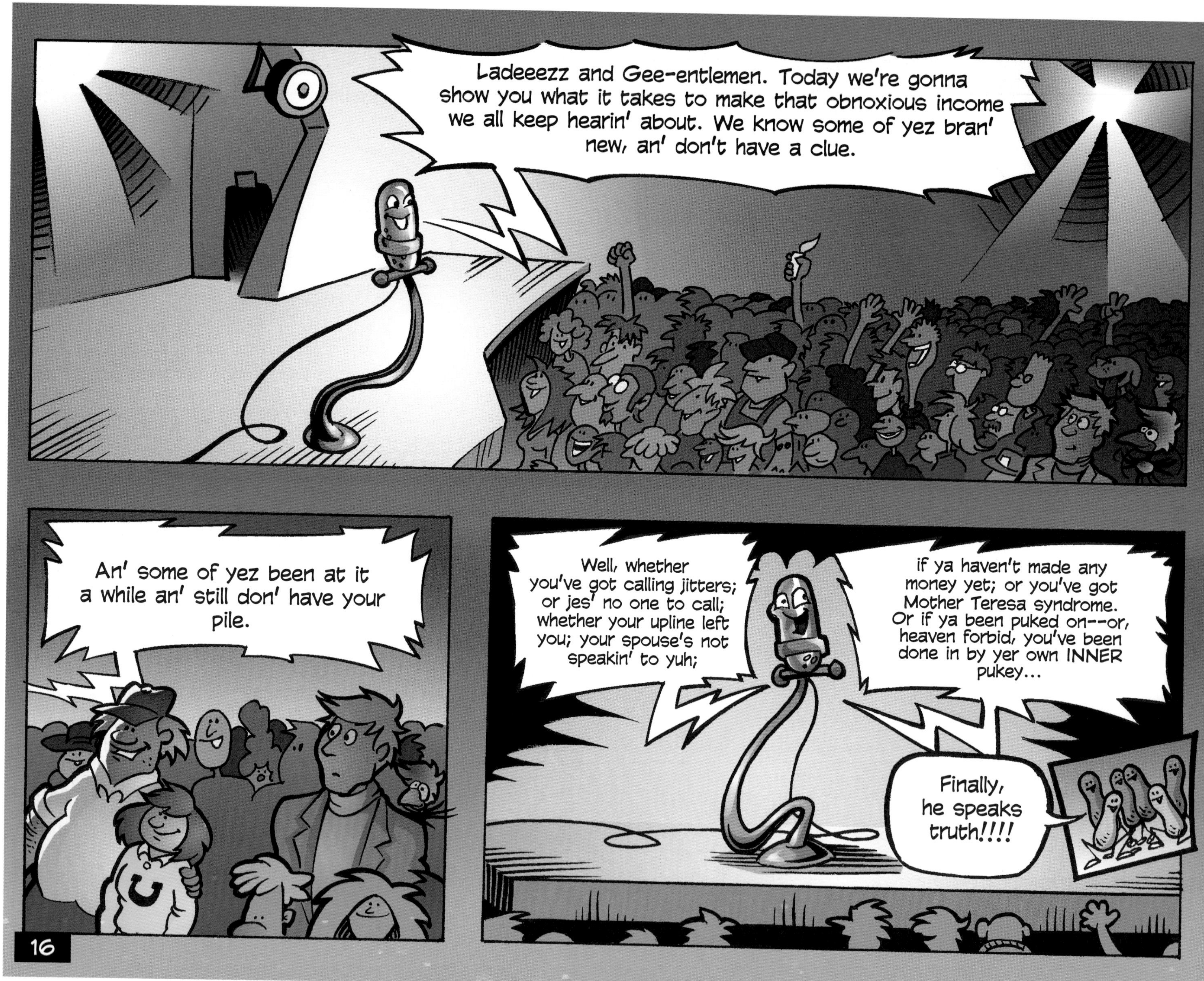
Ladeeezz and Gee-entlemen. Today we're gonna show you what it takes to make that obnoxious income we all keep hearin' about. We know some of yez bran' new, an' don't have a clue.
An' some of yez been at it a while an' still don' have your pile.
Well, whether you've got calling jitters; or jes' no one to call; whether your upline left you; your spouse's not speakin' to yuh;
if ya haven't made any money yet; or you've got Mother Teresa syndrome. Or if ya been puked on--or, heaven forbid, you've been done in by yer own INNER pukey...
Finally, he speaks truth!!!!

...or yer havin' to drag everyone with you across the finish line or worse- -havin' tuh drag yerself over the line. For A-W-W-L-L of these and more, relax, be happy, 'cuz we've got the cure! Ms. Stud! is here and she's gonna tell you The Truth...

What it really takes to make it in Network Marketing!
Yeah, that's it!! We want The Truth. Now!!! We wannit now!!
I feel much better now, don'tchoo? I mean, if it's so easy, how come the place is packed with people trying to figure it out?
Woo Woo! YEAH!
NOW!! NOWWWW!!!
Gosh...I thought it was just me! I was fixing to quit before I came here 'cuz I haven't been able to get ANYBODY yet!

For all people everywhere who are ready to make a change. To make the world a better place with your business or product, here is your mission:
Find people for whom this is the right thing to be doing. No one else. People who have the brains to appreciate the things that you offer.
Of course, there's a trick to successfully completing your mission:
Yeah, I knew it! I'm just as good as those other people--NOW I'm gonna get those little secrets and tricks--so I can get rich, too.
You've got to survive all the wrong ones. They're everywhere. Verily verily I tell you now: They will litter your path. Some of them will be members of the puke set, others will be forever maybes, wrong shoes and yeah yeah do-nothings.
So that's what they call those guys that were so mean to me.
pukeeez!!

Did anybody ever tell you that 90% of the people you'll come across are not right for the business? 'Course they all tell you they need more money and free time. But only 5-10% of them will actually do something to change their situation. So sorry. And, many people just refuse to try your thing--no matter what it is or how much they need it. Anybody ever tell you that?
How many of them do you think there are?
Which ones?
Well that explains it!! I figured for SURE that everybody would say 'yes'. Everybody I know needs money, and the product too...and they wouldn't even listen!
Nobody tole me they wuz gonna puke an' all, did they you?
No! Scumbags!! Holding out on us like that!! No wonder we're having so much trouble!
Since the puke setters are the #1 killer of new babies in the business, let's fix that first.
So what's a pukey?
Yeah, let's get em!
Sounds dizzgusting!!
A pukey is somebody who belittles your new idea, and you, as soon as they hear about it. Before they know anything firsthand. They insult, they sneer, they scoff and ridicule. And often, the better they know you, the worse it is.

I hate to tell ya this, but uhh, pukies also pass pukey germs. And they're wildly infectious.
Germs?? They let off pukey germs?? Oh no! Not that!! Arrgghhhh!!!
It's contagious? How do you...
You mean like a big fat sneeze? With pukey dust sprayed all around? And then we catch it?
I get it now!! That's why I felt so depressed after talking to my uncle! I must've caught some from him.
Nobody tells anybody. So I'm tellin' you now.
Zop

It's not just you, either. Pukeys have plagued the world forever. From the highest echelons to the very bottom.
"Because of his impatience with all who were slow to be convinced, Columbus was considered a little touched in the head...a fool to some and a bore to most... and the worst of it was, he had to persuade stupid people in high places that his enterprise was plausible...because he wanted money, men and equipment."
Christopher Columbus, Mariner by Samuel Eliot Morison,
Columbus petitioned the governments of Portugal, France and Spain for 7 years before Spain's Queen Isabella finally backed him.
oh, ok.
"People give ear to an upstart astrologer who strove to show that the earth revolves, not the heavens,...the sun and the moon...This fool wishes to reverse the entire science of astronomy..."
MARTIN LUTHER, 1533
COSMOS
EARTH
Luther came unglued because the great astronomer Copernicus suggested that the earth was not the center of the universe, and that it moved around the sun.
A former Catholic priest, Martin Luther broke away from the Catholic Church to start his own denomination, because he believed different, new stuff from what the church taught.
Luther's specialty was religion ('how to get to heaven') but he had zero training in scientific theory ('how the heavens go'). Copernicus was right...and Luther was, well, completely wrong.
Remind me of that story next time I get loud or pukey.
OK, I'll say 'what if it does work?'.

Many, many people dumped on Copernicus for his new ideas. And because of it, he almost didn't make it.
100 years later Galileo complained about it too.
"...the scorn which I had to fear on account of the newness and absurdity of my opinion almost drove me to abandon a work already undertaken."
COPERNICUS, 1533
"...I argue not against condemning (Copernicus') book, but against condemning it in the way they suggest--that is, without understanding it, weighing it, or so much as reading it..."
Galileo, 1615 in his Letter to the Grand Duchess Christina

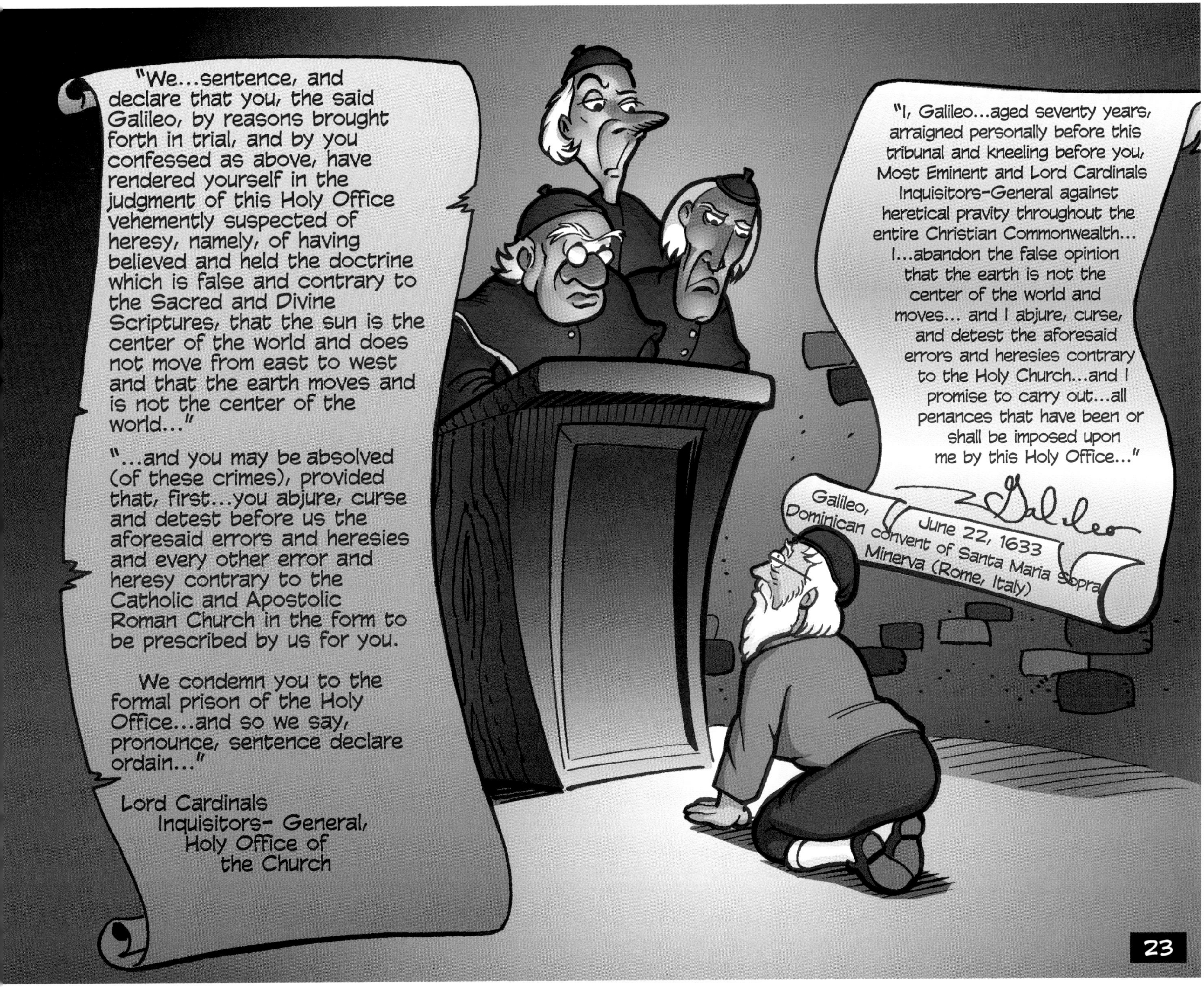
"We...sentence, and declare that you, the said Galileo, by reasons brought forth in trial, and by you confessed as above, have rendered yourself in the judgment of this Holy Office vehemently suspected of heresy, namely, of having believed and held the doctrine which is false and contrary to the Sacred and Divine Scriptures, that the sun is the center of the world and does not move from east to west and that the earth moves and is not the center of the world..."
"...and you may be absolved (of these crimes), provided that, first...you abjure, curse and detest before us the aforesaid errors and heresies and every other error and heresy contrary to the Catholic and Apostolic Roman Church in the form to be prescribed by us for you.
We condemn you to the formal prison of the Holy Office...and so we say, pronounce, sentence declare ordain..."
Lord Cardinals Inquisitors- General, Holy Office of the Church
"I, Galileo...aged seventy years, arraigned personally before this tribunal and kneeling before you, Most Eminent and Lord Cardinals Inquisitors-General against heretical pravity throughout the entire Christian Commonwealth... I...abandon the false opinion that the earth is not the center of the world and moves... and I abjure, curse, and detest the aforesaid errors and heresies contrary to the Holy Church...and I promise to carry out...all penances that have been or shall be imposed upon me by this Holy Office..."
Galileo
Galileo, June 22, 1633
Dominican convent of Santa Maria Sopra Minerva (Rome, Italy)

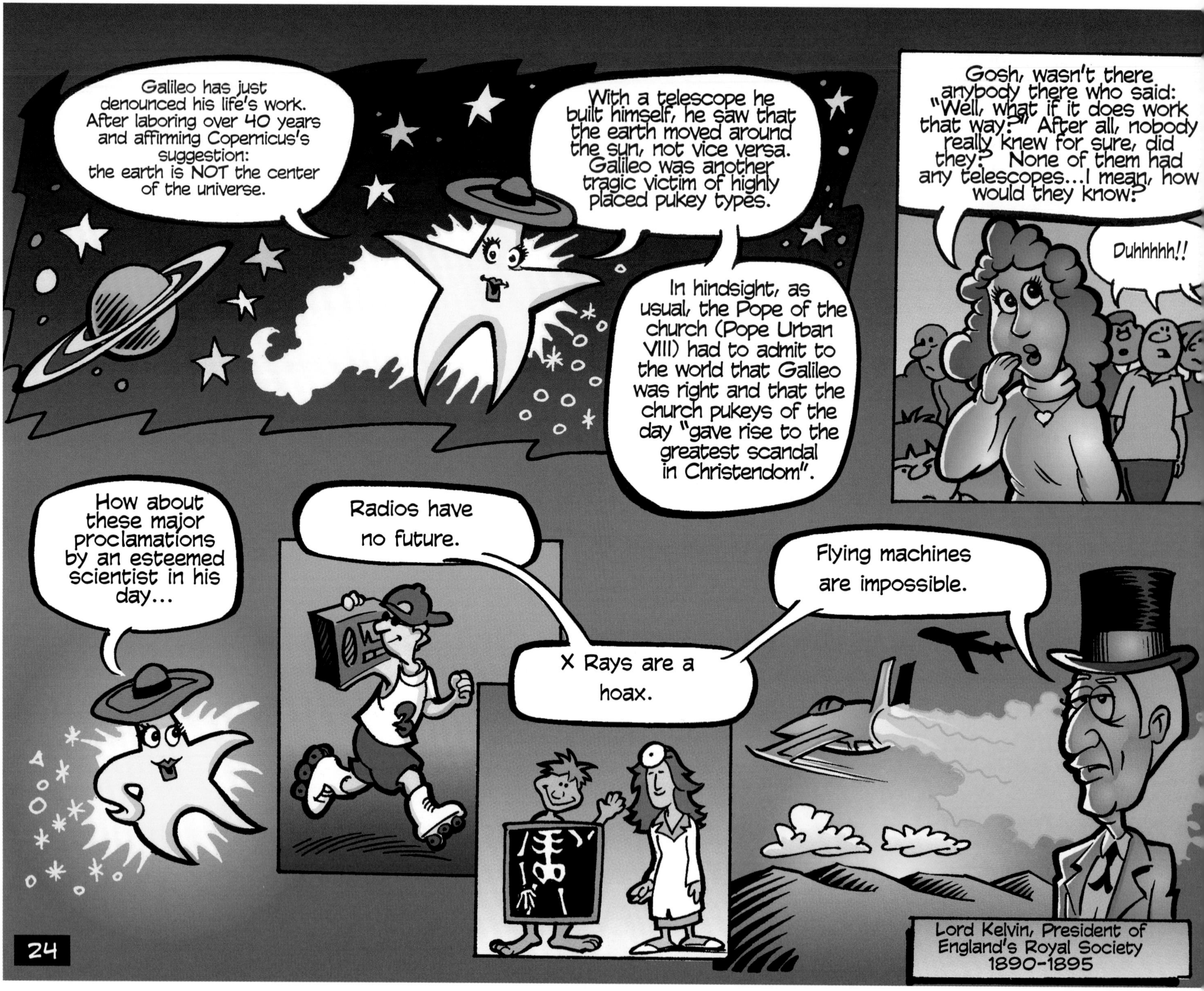
Galileo has just denounced his life's work. After laboring over 40 years and affirming Copernicus's suggestion: the earth is NOT the center of the universe.
With a telescope he built himself, he saw that the earth moved around the sun, not vice versa. Galileo was another tragic victim of highly placed pukey types.
In hindsight, as usual, the Pope of the church (Pope Urban VIII) had to admit to the world that Galileo was right and that the church pukeys of the day "gave rise to the greatest scandal in Christendom".
Gosh, wasn't there anybody there who said: "Well, what if it does work that way?" After all, nobody really knew for sure, did they? None of them had any telescopes...I mean, how would they know?
Duhhhhh!!
How about these major proclamations by an esteemed scientist in his day...
Radios have no future.
X Rays are a hoax.
Flying machines are impossible.
Lord Kelvin, President of England's Royal Society 1890-1895

"...a self promoting humbug." "Sheer nonsense..."
The scientific establishment and newspapers were writing about Thomas Edison, mid 1879, and his likelihood of success inventing the light bulb. On New Year's Eve six months later, Edison lit up a city block before hundreds of writers and thousands of bystanders with 100+ light bulbs. (in Menlo Park, New Jersey).
"...friends and relatives (may) forecast your ruin. In my case, my accountant and lawyer both warned me, 'for my own good' to abort my plans to go into business. They pleaded, 'Mary Kay, don't throw away your life's savings (of $5k). You know nothing about the cosmetics business,'...they even sent me a pamphlet from Washington D.C., stating how many cosmetics companies went out of business everyday. Had I listened to their advice, MKC would have never opened its doors." Mary Kay Ashe, founder of Mary Kay Cosmetics a direct sales company with over 400k independent representatives, in her book, You Can Have it All. p. 87

The top people in your companies also had to endure pukeys before, during and even AFTER they've become wildly successful!! Ask 'em.
For the first 8 years of my network marketing career, I couldn't even say my company's name. People's perceptions of network marketing and the company I represented then--Amway--was so bad. They'd say, 'You're gonna give up teaching at the university to sell soap?'
Even today, Amway people don't say 'Amway'! They're afraid people won't come check it out. When I was there, we all survived by listening to tape after tape of people's horror stories about the pukies and how they kept on despite them. Those years made me what I am...puke proof, as Kim would say.

Paula Pritchard, 22 year network marketing vet. climbed to the top of 4 major companies (Amway, Herbalife, NSA and Quorum.)

Are you still selling those water filters?
1990, Sarasota, FLA. Waiters at the restaurant where NSA's #1 producer, Jeff Roberti, used to work,the day he dropped by in his new Ferrari, after having earned $6million already!
Cafe

You'll be back.
When that fails,
you'll be back.
Thanks a lot, dad.
Thanks.
Darren Hardy, top producer in the industry, with dad, Jerry, leaving to start his networking career.
Dad hoped to lure him back to his real estate business.
Formerly #1 earner with TPN, now front line independent rep with Pre-Paid Legal.
Finally, get this:
A January, 1998 comment by an unnamed multimedia design firm owner to Max Out Production's Paula English (our project designer).
You don't understand this business. You'll never get artists to work on this project with you. Professional cartoonists don't work alongside writers. You'll never get this project off the ground.

What could I DO if I did run into the big pukeys? I'm not very brave. Not yet, anyway.
I don't know if I could stand very many pukey types doing that to me.
Yeah, why did God make so many of them, anyway?
Well, you don't have to take it anymore. What if you got to say 'NO' to them first? How would that be?
Huh? Did she say blow 'em off first?
How would you do that?
Yes. So you don't catch their pukey germs.
But what if you only know a few people? If I say 'no' first to them, what'll I do for people to talk to?
And what if they really NEED the product? Shouldn't we just MAKE 'EM do it?
3-10 pukes and you're out, remember... babies too.

But what if some of them change their minds later?
Did you know you can always go back to anyone later?
True...good. I'll keep a 'later' list then...in case they change their minds. After all, what if they do?
Wanna see how to say 'NO' first? To you know who?
Yes!! Yes!! Let's do it!! Let's see it!!
Yeah, let's see doin' Jerry, huh?

OK. I've brought along a world renowned specialist. He can say 'no' first to anyone, anytime, and in any way that seems right. He can even match or beat the attitude of the culprit being pukey.
Come awwwwwn out!
Where was he when I needed him?
May I introduce...
ZAYNO FURST!!!
Where're the pukies? Show me the pukies! Take me to your pukies and whinies now!!
Can he do it to mine? Can he do it to mine?

ZAYNO FURST is available to anyone of you--all ya gotta do is ask. He's always ready to do his name. Wanna see him do his thing?
Where are the pukeys? Where are the pukeys?
Can he do it to mine? Can he do it to mine?
ZōP

Right there!! Right there!!
I wonder what he'll do...
He does his name!!! He does his name!!!!

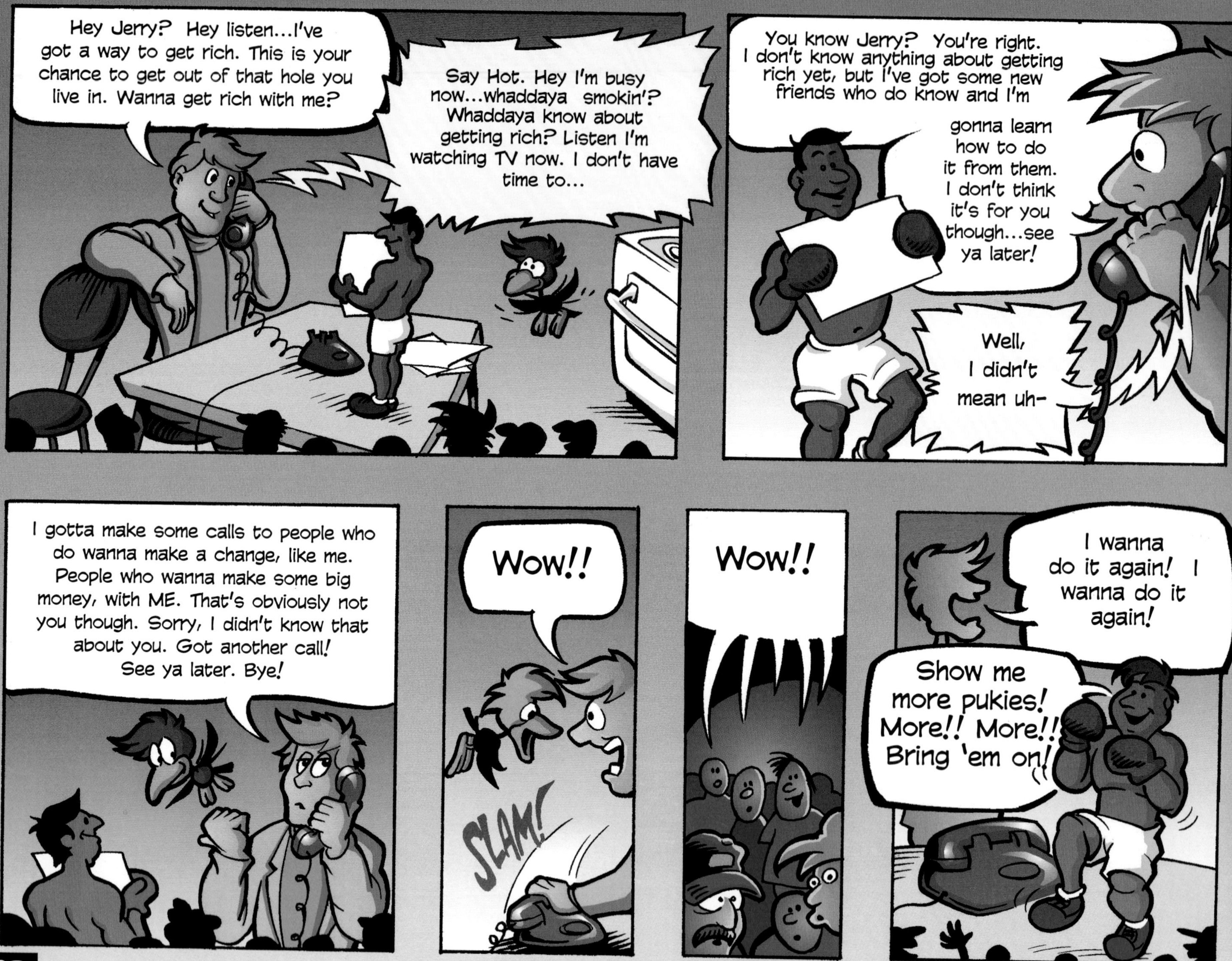

Hey Jerry? Hey listen...I've got a way to get rich. This is your chance to get out of that hole you live in. Wanna get rich with me?
Say Hot. Hey I'm busy now...whaddaya smokin'? Whaddaya know about getting rich? Listen I'm watching TV now. I don't have time to...
You know Jerry? You're right. I don't know anything about getting rich yet, but I've got some new friends who do know and I'm gonna learn how to do it from them. I don't think it's for you though...see ya later!
Well, I didn't mean uh-
I gotta make some calls to people who do wanna make a change, like me. People who wanna make some big money, with ME. That's obviously not you though. Sorry, I didn't know that about you. Got another call! See ya later. Bye!
Wow!!
SLAM!
Wow!!
I wanna do it again! I wanna do it again!
Show me more pukies! More!! More!! Bring 'em on!

Uncle Donald? Yess, I've started my own business and I was wondering if you knew anyone who might like to earn some extra income from home, and help make people healthier at the same time.
Your own business? They took you for a sucker, that's for sure. Whadya go to school for all those years? Can'tcha get a real job?
Lemme at 'im! Lemme at 'im!
You can't make any money with them things...What's wrong with you?
You know Uncle Donald, I made a mistake calling you. There's this lady who's very successful--and she said there'd be pukey types who'd dump on this without knowing anything about it. I didn't think it would be you, though.
Pukey type? I'm not a pukey type! Listen Hot...
I am not a pukey! Listen Hot...
Talk to you later!!!
Well, 'hello' to Aunt Martha...I gotta go...another call...bye!

Way cool!!!! I think maybe I can do that. Could I see you do ONE more, then I'll try the next one after that, ok?
Show me the pukies! Show me the whinies!
Go baby!!!! Go baby go!!!!

Hey Joe. Hey listen-
-if I could show you a way to get healthy and make big money at the same time, and it could fit into your schedule, would you wanna check it out?
Uhhh...I don't know. Is it one of those things? Would I have to spend my own money? How much would you make on me?
You know Joe, you're right. I'm talking about starting a business of your own. I don't think it's something you could do...
Uh, well...
...You'll have to put out somethun'...some time, some money, some imagination--and for sure--good energy. I don't think this is something you could do. It's ok, you stay the way you are.
Uh, uhh. Well maybe-
Listen, I'll talk to you later...got another call...bye!

I think I can do that. We'll practice it together.
Will you be there forever? Until I can do it by myself?
Forever, forever.
Yeah baby!! He's comin' home with us!! Till I can do it myself!
Yeah! And then guess who gets him...
My new babies!! They get him...so they can last!!
What about some more?
Sock it to me...Sock it to me! Show me the pukies!

It's too expensive!
You're right, it is too expensive for you, totally out of your league. It's ok though, this is not something for you. Got another call...talk to you later.
I can't sell. And anyway, I don't know anyone.
Well, I can certainly see why! Actually, you're right. If you think you can't, you're right. Henry Ford said that, d'you know that? Hmmmmm? Gotta go--another call!

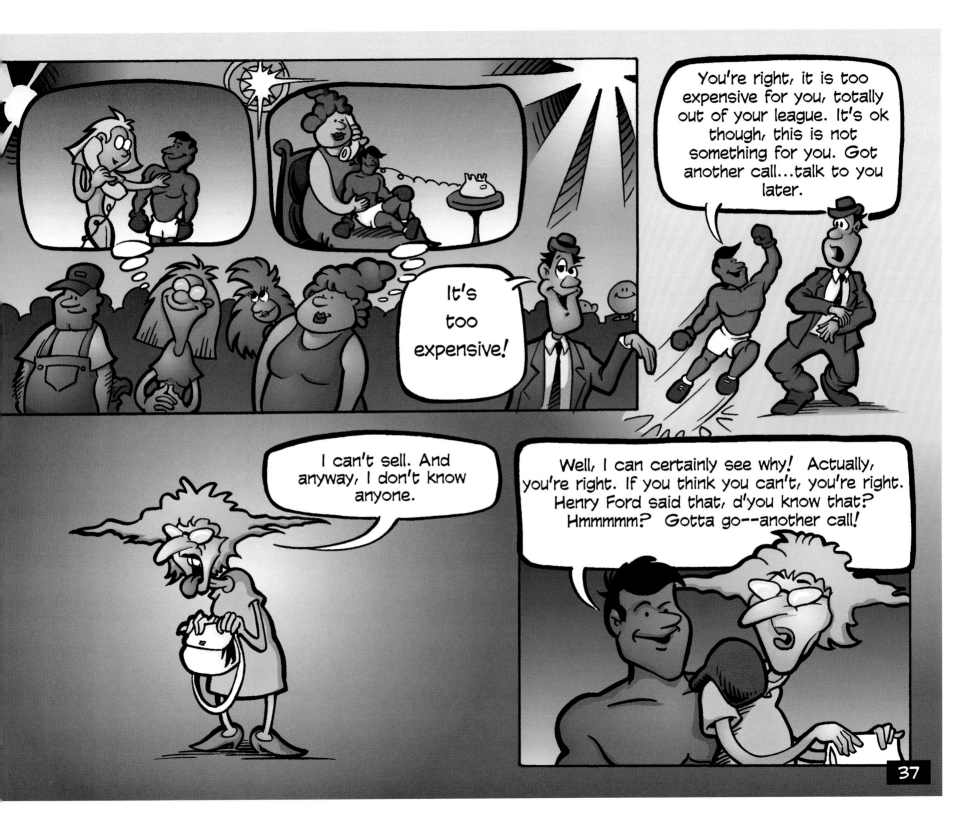

I don't have any time or money and anyway...
Ok. Well you let me know when you're ready to make a change in either of those areas, ok? Gotta go--another call... talk to ya later!
What about the ones who don't really act pukey? They just waffle, and you can't get anywhere with 'em?
They don't say 'no' and don't say 'yes'. But they never do anything.
Oh yeah, the forever maybes. I can do 'em. Where is one?

Well, I'm not sure. Like I said last time, it sounds interesting--but I'm pretty busy. Maybe later...
Well, since we've already talked a couple of times, let's do this: you let me know when you're ready to make a change and DO something about it. I don't wanna be a bug--so you let me know when you're ready. I love ya still, but I'm on a deadline. I'm looking for people that are ready to do something NOW. I'll be here for you whenever, OK?! Gotta go...another call...
Can we do that for people already IN our heap?
Totally. That's the goodbye message. We'll show you how to do that in about 10 minutes.

Well, I'm appalled, aren't you? I think that's just too fast, don't you? Some of those people might come around...
...especially with a little care. This might be a chance for us to help them at a deeper level.
I completely agree. Isn't this a people business? We ought to hold everyone where they could be, and then maybe they might experience internal change, and become what we hold them up to be.
But what if they don't hold themselves the way we do?
With a little time, who knows? After all, not everybody is ready at the same time, are they? I don't think everybody here signed up the first time they heard about it, do you?
Mmmmm. Maybe she's gonna tell us how to decide--you know--how much time and precious energy we should spend with them. And WHEN to spend it.
We'll see.

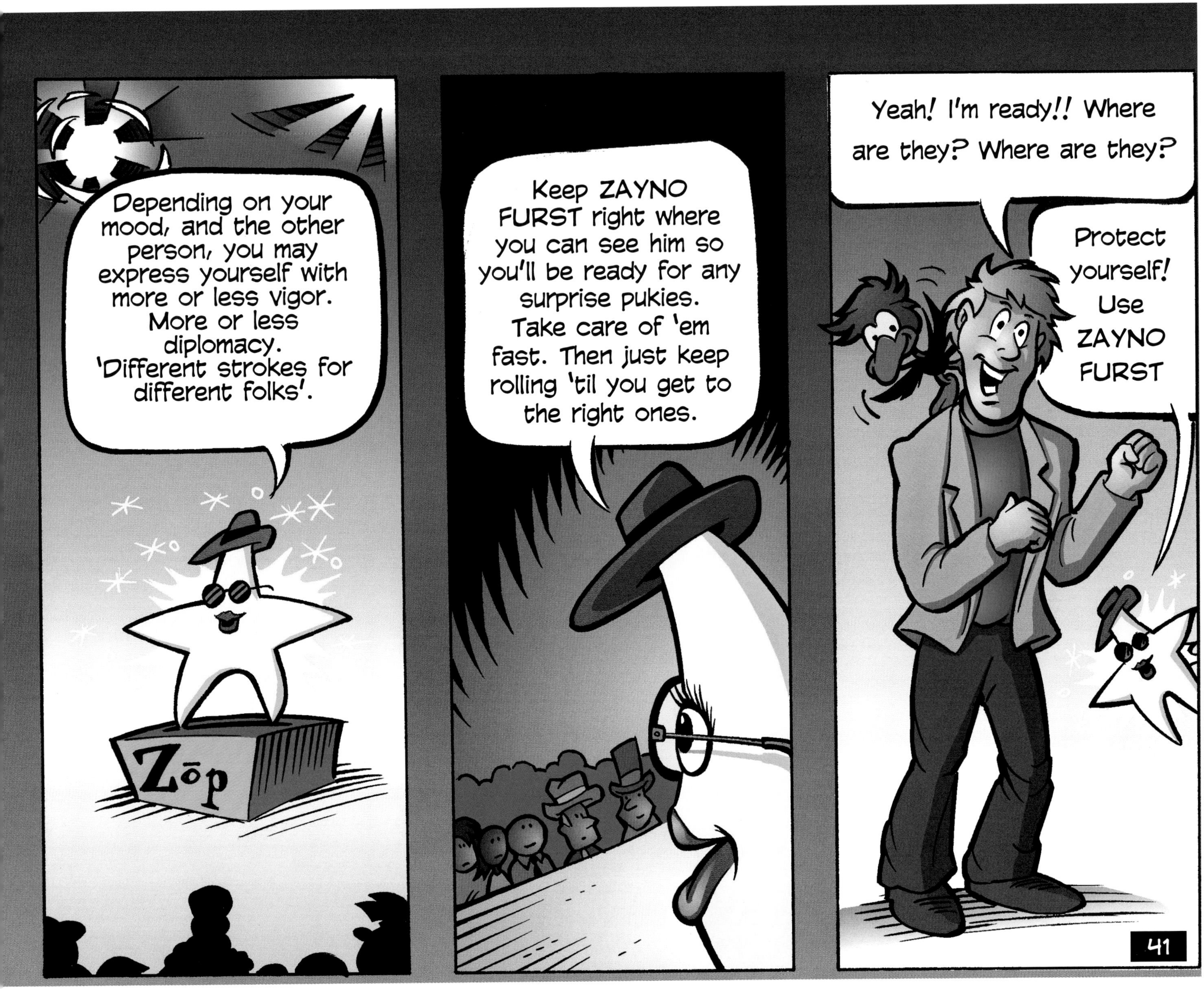
Depending on your mood, and the other person, you may express yourself with more or less vigor. More or less diplomacy. 'Different strokes for different folks'.
Zōp
Keep ZAYNO FURST right where you can see him so you'll be ready for any surprise pukies. Take care of 'em fast. Then just keep rolling 'til you get to the right ones.
Yeah! I'm ready!! Where are they? Where are they?
Protect yourself! Use ZAYNO FURST

This is it! This is the way to build a giant heap! And without those friends, family or neighbors--or ANYBODY! I LOVE THIS!!
Uhhh, yeah. But how do we get more people to say 'no' to? Or say ANYthing to?
Yeah...uhhh, didn't think of that. We're gonna need a lot of people to say 'no' to first, and maybe other stuff. Somebody might say 'yes', if we could just find 'em.

So, where do we get 'em then?

APPLICATION
APPLICATION
APPLICATIONS
Sign-ups Here

Do you believe?
YES!!!
Oooohh, finally!
Uhh, believe what?
I dunno.
We're not going to do all that gooey belief and burning desire stuff now, are we?
ZōP
Do you believe it when they say that 5-10% of the people out there are the right ones?
The 'ones'? What 'ones'?
The ones for whom this is the right thing to be doing? You know, your business or product?
YEEESSS!!!
ZōP

OK then, if there are 5-10% out there somewhere, would you agree that the #1 trick to making it in this business is to last long enough to find them? YES or NO??
YES!!
Alright. Next, do you want to find these people in your life time?
YESSSSS! Of course!! Ha ha ha!
So what's the fastest way to get to them? That is the question, yes?

Well, if you are a highly influential person, and your contacts have big spheres of influence, and people do anything you say...
She means like Madonna, or the Pope, Billy Graham, or Martha Stewart, right?
Yeah!!!
...then you just tell 'em, that's all.
Zip
But what about me? No one I know will listen to me!
Well, take the *Ms. Stud!* AQ Test (Attitude Quotient) to see if you're going as fast as you can. Remember you're looking to find the 5-10% as soon as possible, right?
Ok I'm ready. Will this help me raise my AQ?

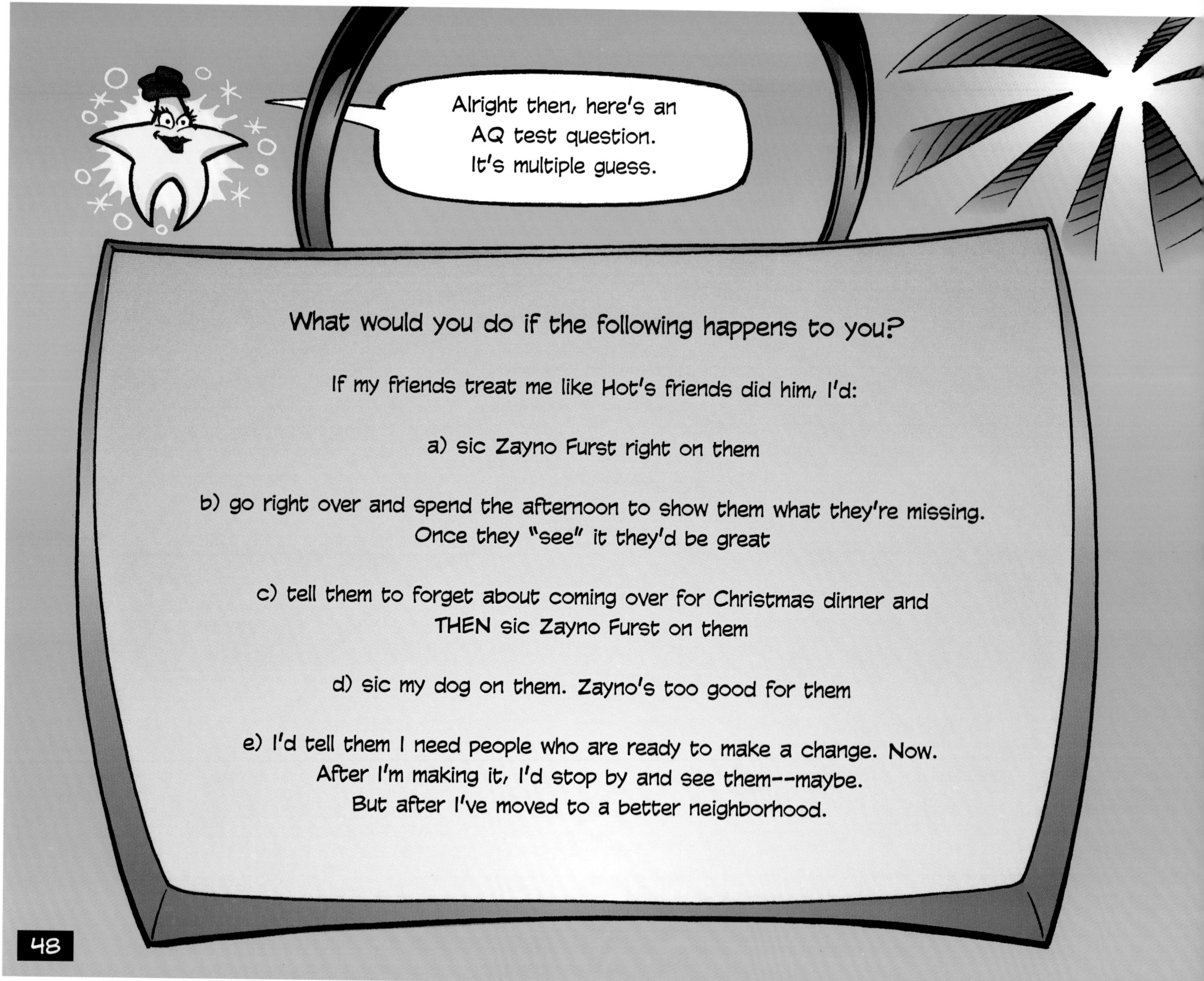
Alright then, here's an AQ test question. It's multiple guess.
What would you do if the following happens to you?
If my friends treat me like Hot's friends did him, I'd:
a) sic Zayno Furst right on them
b) go right over and spend the afternoon to show them what they're missing. Once they "see" it they'd be great
c) tell them to forget about coming over for Christmas dinner and THEN sic Zayno Furst on them
d) sic my dog on them. Zayno's too good for them
e) I'd tell them I need people who are ready to make a change. Now. After I'm making it, I'd stop by and see them--maybe. But after I've moved to a better neighborhood.

I'm doing e). I'm not losing my chance at obscene income because of any dumb friends I have...you?
No way. I'm going to give 'em a chance, but they're not holding ME back. I don't want to end up where they are.
Well, I wanna go SUPER FAST! So I'm doing a) an only a)! I wannit NOW. I wanna make a BIG change. RIGHT eff'n NOW!!
How do we MAKE somebody go fast? Do we just shake 'em or something?
GO FAST!
I'm pretty frail. I don't think I could stand too much abuse or too much pukey stuff. I'll need ZAYNO FURST right with me.
Ok, let's play a game that shows a preview of what's to come. Who wants to volunteer to come up here and play with me?
Everybody gets a deck of cards. OK everybody, how many ACES in a deck of 52 cards?

OK, now, when the gong sounds, race through your decks and find the four Aces. The first one to find their Aces is the winner!
Everybody got it? All cards face down?
FLIP!
Ready?
Set!
Go!

OK. How much time did anybody here spend with the wrong cards?
NONE!!!!!
When they turned up a 3, did anybody go: "Well, this oughta be an Ace--I'm going to fix this one right now!".
WITE OUT
...and then you grabbed the white-out, scratched out the 3, and tried to write over it and make it into an ace?
Ha ha!!! Of course not!! Ha ha ha!!!

Did anyone here do that in the Race for Aces? No? Well why not?
'Cuz it's faster to keep flipping. You KNOW there's an Ace in there somewhere!
Yeah, and who's got time in the race to scratch out 3s and turn 'em into Aces, anyway? Ha ha ha ha!
Are you doing that with people?
Yeow! I've been scratching 3s!!!
I can't believe it...that's what I've been doing all along. But no more!
I wish I'd known this sooner. I'd have gotten past those pukeys faster.
Yeah, me too. From now on I'm searching for Aces.
Aarrgghhhh!!!! I've wasted so much time!

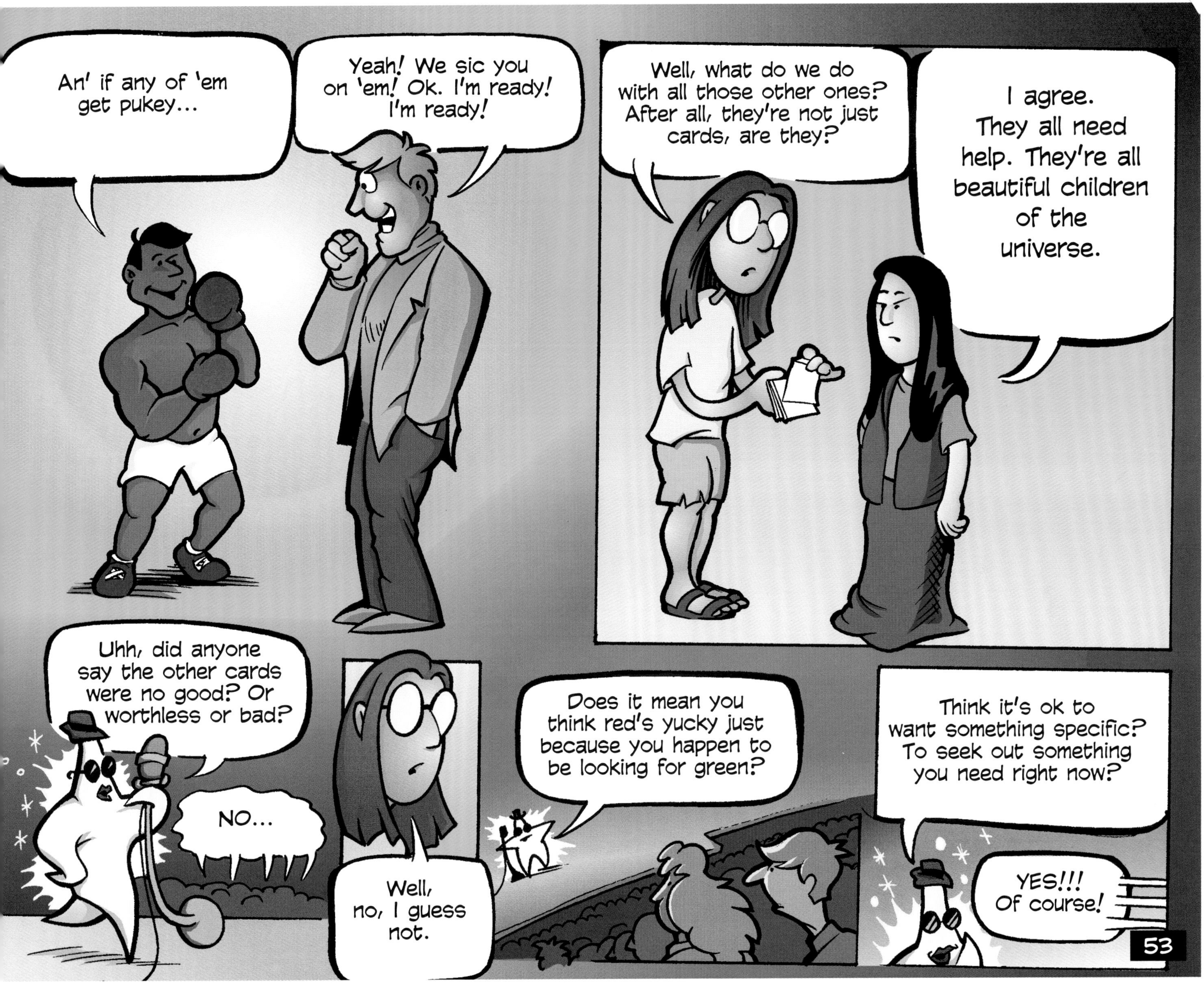
An' if any of 'em get pukey...
Yeah! We sic you on 'em! Ok. I'm ready! I'm ready!
Well, what do we do with all those other ones? After all, they're not just cards, are they?
I agree. They all need help. They're all beautiful children of the universe.
Uhh, did anyone say the other cards were no good? Or worthless or bad?
NO...
Well, no, I guess not.
Does it mean you think red's yucky just because you happen to be looking for green?
Think it's ok to want something specific? To seek out something you need right now?
YES!!! Of course!

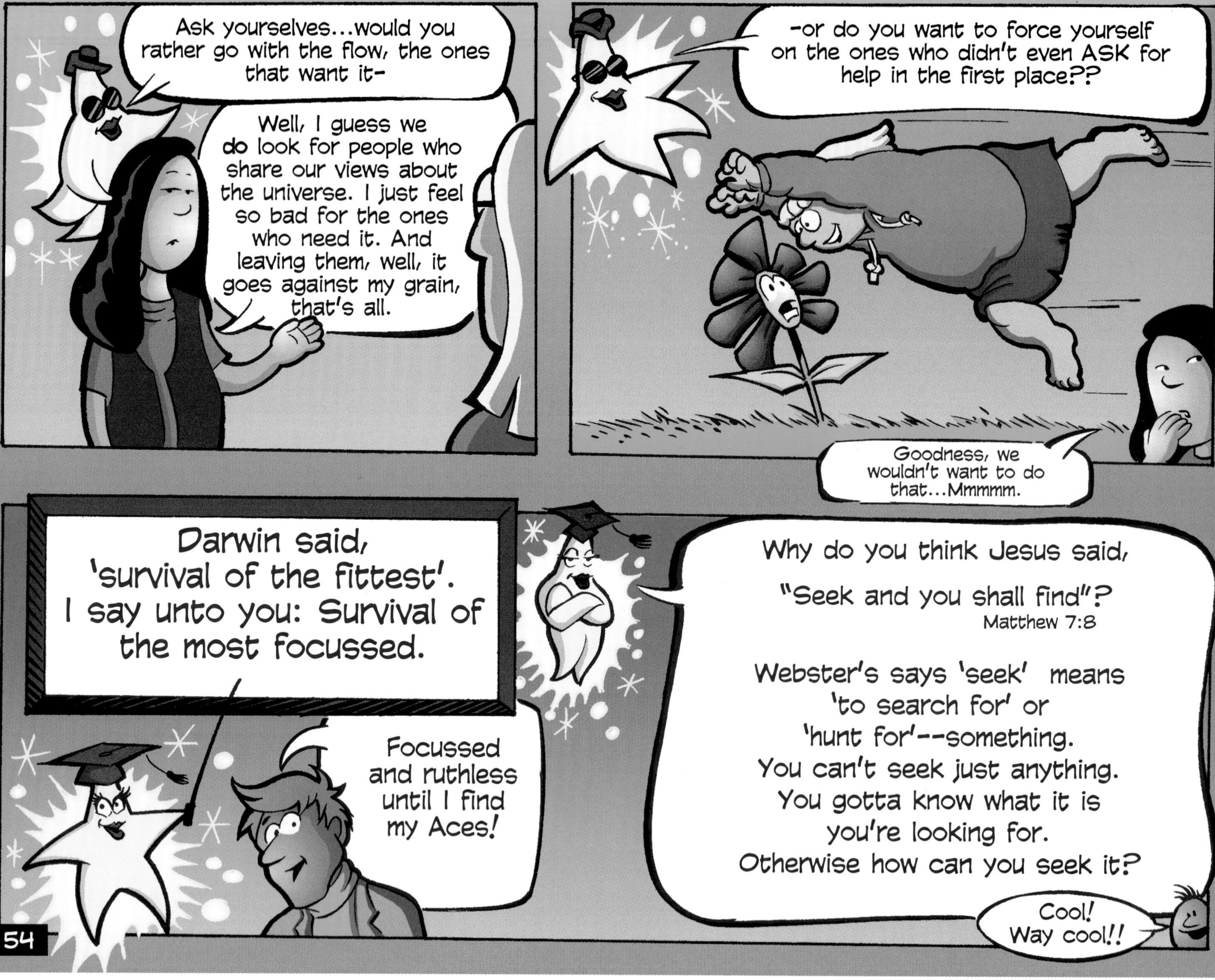
Ask yourselves...would you rather go with the flow, the ones that want it-
Well, I guess we do look for people who share our views about the universe. I just feel so bad for the ones who need it. And leaving them, well, it goes against my grain, that's all.
-or do you want to force yourself on the ones who didn't even ASK for help in the first place??
Goodness, we wouldn't want to do that...Mmmmm.
Darwin said, 'survival of the fittest'. I say unto you: Survival of the most focussed.
Focussed and ruthless until I find my Aces!
Why do you think Jesus said,
"Seek and you shall find"?
Matthew 7:8
Webster's says 'seek' means 'to search for' or 'hunt for'--something. You can't seek just anything. You gotta know what it is you're looking for. Otherwise how can you seek it?
Cool! Way cool!!

Jesus knew that.
No one can begin to 'seek' unless they know what they're seeking.
Bottom line: you cannot use the word 'seek' unless you have the object you're seeking in your mind FIRST, got it?
I got it!!!! Seek Aces and you shall find Aces!! That's my motto from now on!

So, what if you seek out your Aces first? Pass up everything else until you have a team that can help you survive, so you can help others.
Ok. So uhh, what's an Ace, exactly?
Ace: Somebody friendly, ambitious, open minded, willing to learn new tricks and ready to make a change NOW. Must have life force. Obsessive tendencies a plus.
We skip over them other ones so we don't catch their pukey bugs an' maybe come down with it ourselves, right?

You got it! You got it! You got it! Tell your new babies now!
Well, alright, but I'm going to keep a list--for going back later...just in case.
Can't control others, can we?
Remember what flight attendants say to all passengers, on every airline flight hundreds of times EVERY DAY... day in day out, 365 days a year?
In case of big trouble, oxygen masks will drop from the ceiling...put on your own mask FIRST, then help children and people acting like children.
Why do you think they say that?

How many people can you REALLY help if you've become a statistic yourself because you were scratching 3s when the clock ran out?
And then you get too many pukey germs and self-destruct, right?
What good are you to others if you're already dead, right?
I'm glad somebody told me this now. I'm NEVER going to stop flipping till I get my Aces, no matter what. And I'm tellin' my babies the same thing. What about you?
Yeah. That's what I'm telling them all. Don't stop...don't stop...don't stop... keep on flippin'...keep on flippin'. We just **know** there are Aces in there somewhere! What if it does work, right?

Some people keep a big 'later' list--so they can go back to the 3s and 5s later. After you've got your Aces in tow.
Why yes, and maybe one or two of them might even be ready to make a change by then, who knows? Maybe they'll have turned themselves into an Ace somehow!
Yeah. Think that's how that happens with real people?
I dunno. Maybe for some of them. It's probably worth checking back, AFTER we've got it together tho'. I don't wanna spend any time now scratchin' 3s.
Yeaahhh... Aces first. I got it!
Why, I feel much better now. I can visualize a beautiful charity for all the lost children of the universe...after we're successful.
Why yes!! With OUR name on it!
Y'know I do remember reading somewhere what Abe Lincoln said about the poor-
Oh, what? He was soooo truly compassionate.
-he said the best thing we can do for the poor is to NOT join them.
Mmm, yes. Well, that's why we're here, right?
CAPS

OK I'm ready. So how do we do this race? Where are the decks of people? I'm ready to start flippin'!
Do you think there's going to be enough, uhh, 'decks' for all of us?
EXIT
Here's our people map of the U.S. Give or take, there are about 200 million people here.
7-11 million* of these people have already signed an app for one or another network marketing company.
*according to Professor Charles W. King Harvard University, Doctor of Business Admin. Chiropractic Economics, Vol. 40 #2
Oh no!!! Are we too late?
Course not! Lookit all the ones that are still left!!!
7 to 11 MILLION Signed up
Of the 7-11 mil sign-ups, just a tiny percentage are serious business builders...the ones making the obscene income. Thousands upon thousands are part time builders looking for that elusive 'better deal'.

Why's everyone looking?
Because they didn't get what they expected when they first signed up. For starters, they had no clue what would befall them when they started hitting up you know who.
Ooohh...no one told them either? Ain't it jus' awwwful?
But look at the bright side...
...when so many people are unhappy, there's always good news.
There is? What???
Most of them are looking--to join a team they can be a part of.
Ah ha!! So that means they're free agents, right? We can start our own team!
Might go faster too, if we get some of them!! Bein' experienced an' all! So where are they?
I gotta warn you, the 80-20 rule is alive and well for those people too, just like it is everywhere in the world.
I knew it. Here comes the big bomb.
What 80-20 rule?
20% of the people are responsible for 80% of the business, 80% of the results and 80% of the money that's generated.

So what's with those other people?
Some are future 20%ers. Others are wannabes, followers, supporters, hangers-on, me-toos, some yeah-yeah do-nothings, forever maybes and even puke setters.
Puke setters? Even IN the heap?
Hate to break it to you, but yes, puke setters IN the heap. We'll show you how to get rid of them or neutralize them, so don't worry.
Be happy!!
So back to the big Q: are there enough people out there?
Remember we said that 5-10% of the people are the right ones?
That means, theoretically 10-20 million people are the right ones for your business or product...and LOTS of them even have some experience!
Wow!! 10-20 million!! All 'right ones'?

We wannem all!! How can we getum all?
Ok ok. I believe already! There are LOTS of right ones out there. So how many do I need to make the big money?
She said just a few...should be a piece of cake!
Yeah, but don'tcha think everybody else in the world will be lookin' for the Aces too? People from all those other deals?
I want the Geiger counter. Where's the Geiger counter to find the Aces?
Hmmmm...well, we'll just hafta figure out how to get to them FIRST, that's all.
Here's the good news: You only need a few good ones. Think Jesus...
...he only had 12, and now look! One quarter of the world's population is in his group!
Gee yeah!! I never thought about that.
Uhh, cool. But who's got 2,000 years to get the whole world!??
Today, you can reach just as many people in a single weekend. Gazillions in days!
Awwrrrighttttt!!!!! And we only need a few good ones!
SMACK!

Did you know most top earners have only 2-4 big stud types? And that 85% or more of their income comes from those 2-4?
Like Jesus, a very small band of committed believers.
And one of the 12 guys was a major pukey--front line, even!!

And even with the big pukey, that tiny band impacted thousands upon thousands of others--who impacted thousands and thousands of others, who continue to tell the story today.
Most big players do it with 2-4 key people...who do it with 2-4, who do it with 2-4, who do it with 2-4.
How can they do all that with only 2-4 'stud-types'? I gotta meet these guys.

Here's straight from some of my studley friends...
Hi! I'm Dr. Matt Silver, independent rep for FreeLife. I have over 15,000 people in my down line. I went to people I knew at first.
Well that explains it! I'm not an MD! He probably got other stud MD types with huge practices and of course they all said yes! Not even one pukey, I bet!
Cool! How many front line people did you sponsor?
Uhh, about 18.
And how many of those flaked,?
Uhh, about 8. I've got 10 front line people that are active.
See, how can I do that? He knows other MDs, that's why!
Matt Silver, MD
FreeLife Int'l rep

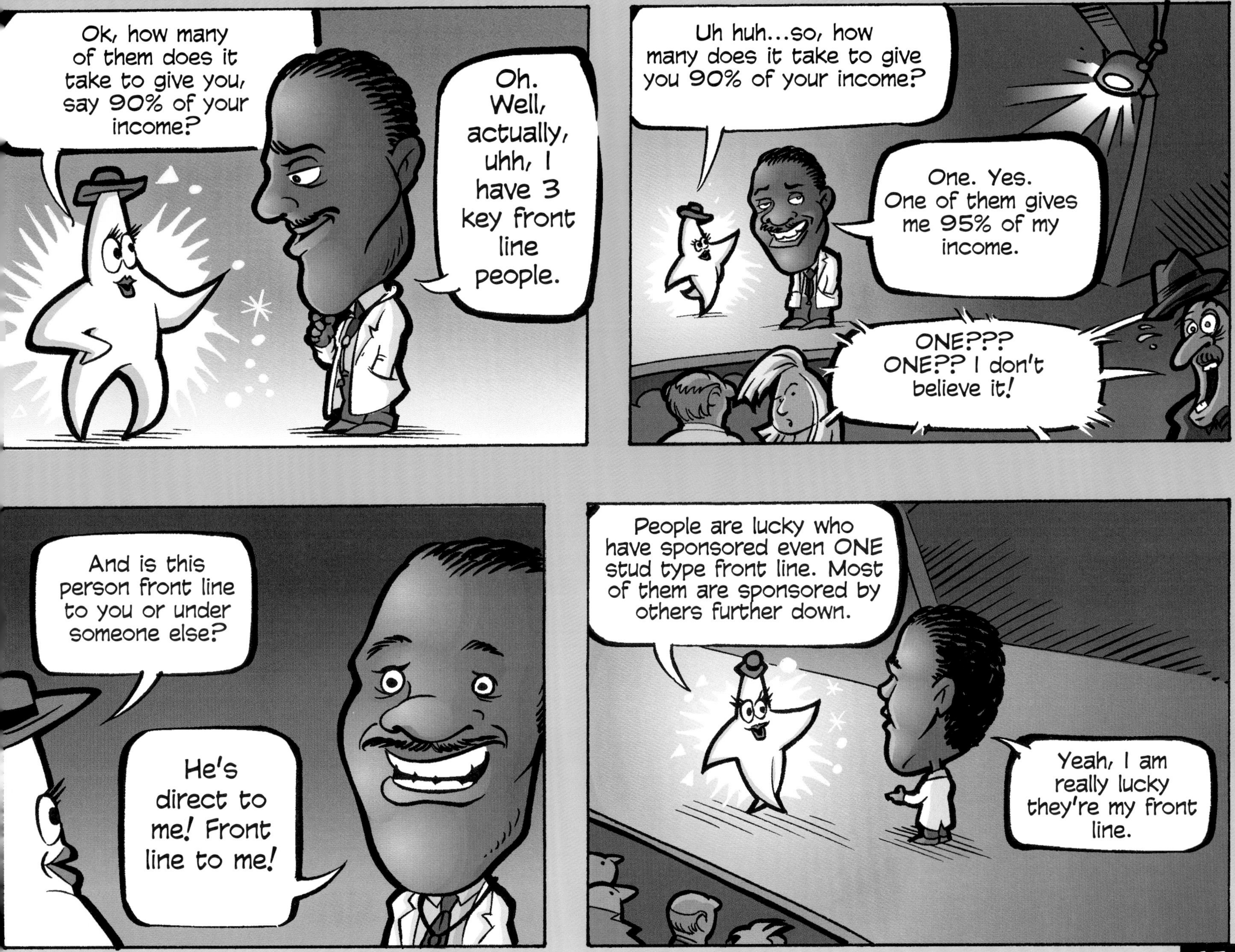
Ok, how many of them does it take to give you, say 90% of your income?
Oh. Well, actually, uhh, I have 3 key front line people.
Uh huh...so, how many does it take to give you 90% of your income?
One. Yes. One of them gives me 95% of my income.
ONE??? ONE?? I don't believe it!
And is this person front line to you or under someone else?
He's direct to me! Front line to me!
People are lucky who have sponsored even ONE stud type front line. Most of them are sponsored by others further down.
Yeah, I am really lucky they're my front line.

So how did you meet this person? How did you sponsor them?
Well uhh, actually, he was a referral from someone else. I knew him though, and he wanted to come in under me.
So how'd you get him?
Well, my upline talked to him first. Then he discovered we knew each other. My wonderful upline let the prospect choose. He could sign up direct to my upline or direct to me. My friend chose me! Cool, huh?
Wow! Gosh! Lucky guy!!!
Way cool. Uhh, how long did it take to make some big money?
In a year and a half, I surpassed the income from my medical practice. Well over 5 figures a month.
Wow!!!!! In only a year and a half!!! I'm ready, I wanna do that, too!
Uhh, five figures a month...that means $10,000 or more, right?
So was this your first networking deal?
Heavens no!! I'd been doing it for 13 years part time before I got involved with FreeLife.
That explains it. Maybe I can do it in less than 13 years.
Oh...
Yeah.

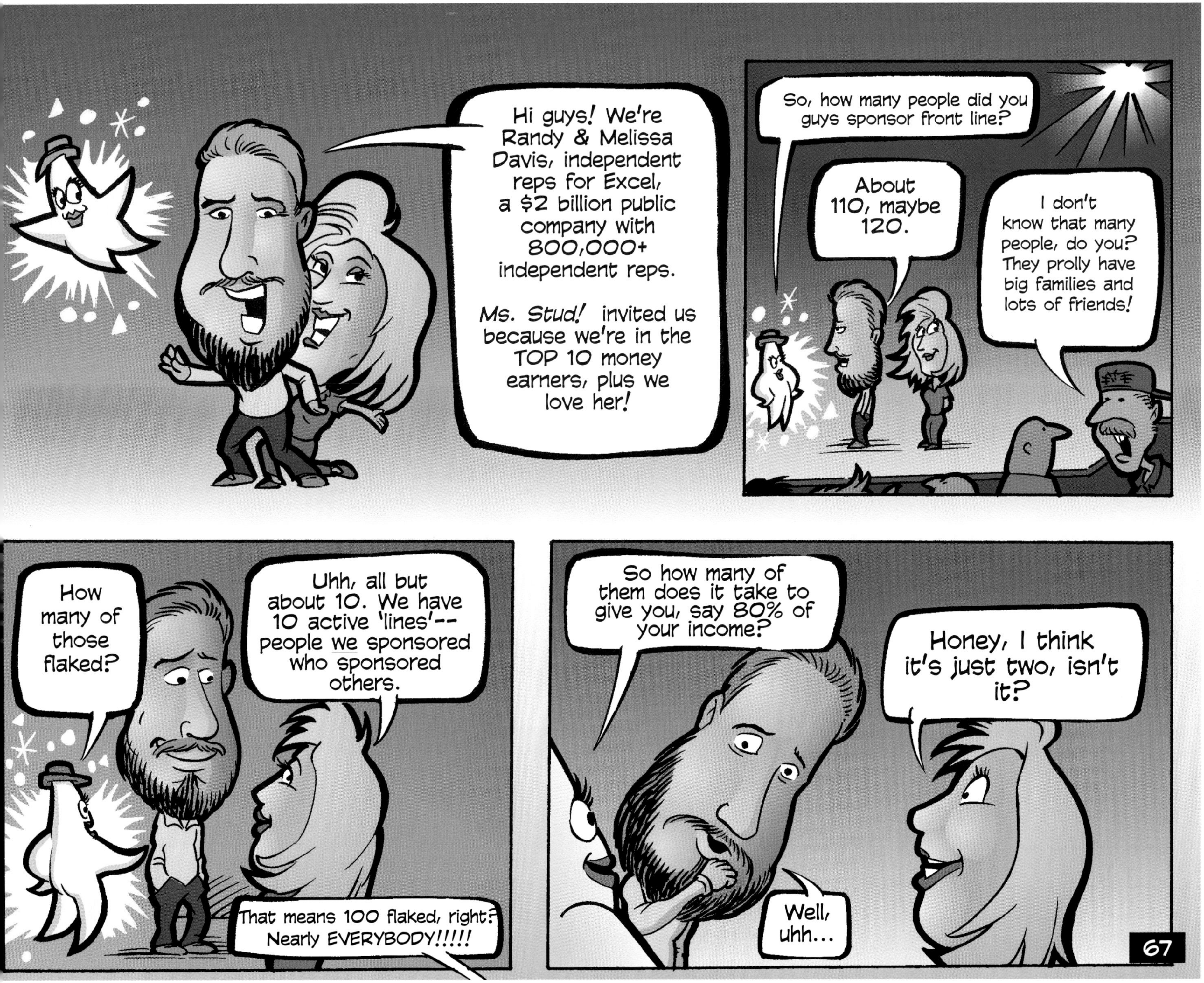

Hi guys! We're Randy & Melissa Davis, independent reps for Excel, a $2 billion public company with 800,000+ independent reps.
Ms. Stud! invited us because we're in the TOP 10 money earners, plus we love her!
So, how many people did you guys sponsor front line?
About 110, maybe 120.
I don't know that many people, do you? They prolly have big families and lots of friends!
How many of those flaked?
Uhh, all but about 10. We have 10 active 'lines'--people we sponsored who sponsored others.
That means 100 flaked, right? Nearly EVERYBODY!!!!!
So how many of them does it take to give you, say 80% of your income?
Well, uhh...
Honey, I think it's just two, isn't it?

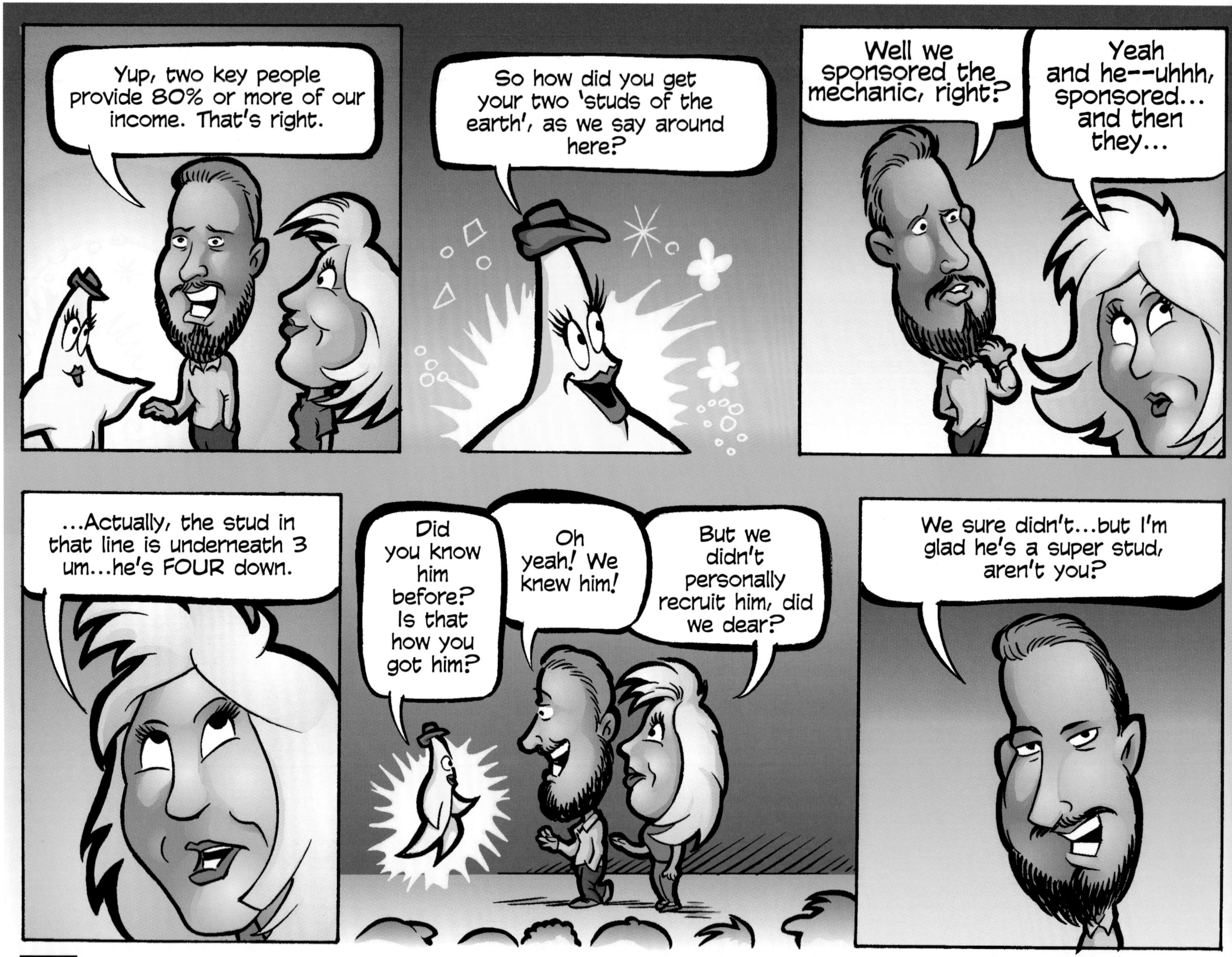
Yup, two key people provide 80% or more of our income. That's right.
So how did you get your two 'studs of the earth', as we say around here?
Well we sponsored the mechanic, right?
Yeah and he--uhhh, sponsored... and then they...
...Actually, the stud in that line is underneath 3 um...he's FOUR down.
Did you know him before? Is that how you got him?
Oh yeah! We knew him!
But we didn't personally recruit him, did we dear?
We sure didn't...but I'm glad he's a super stud, aren't you?

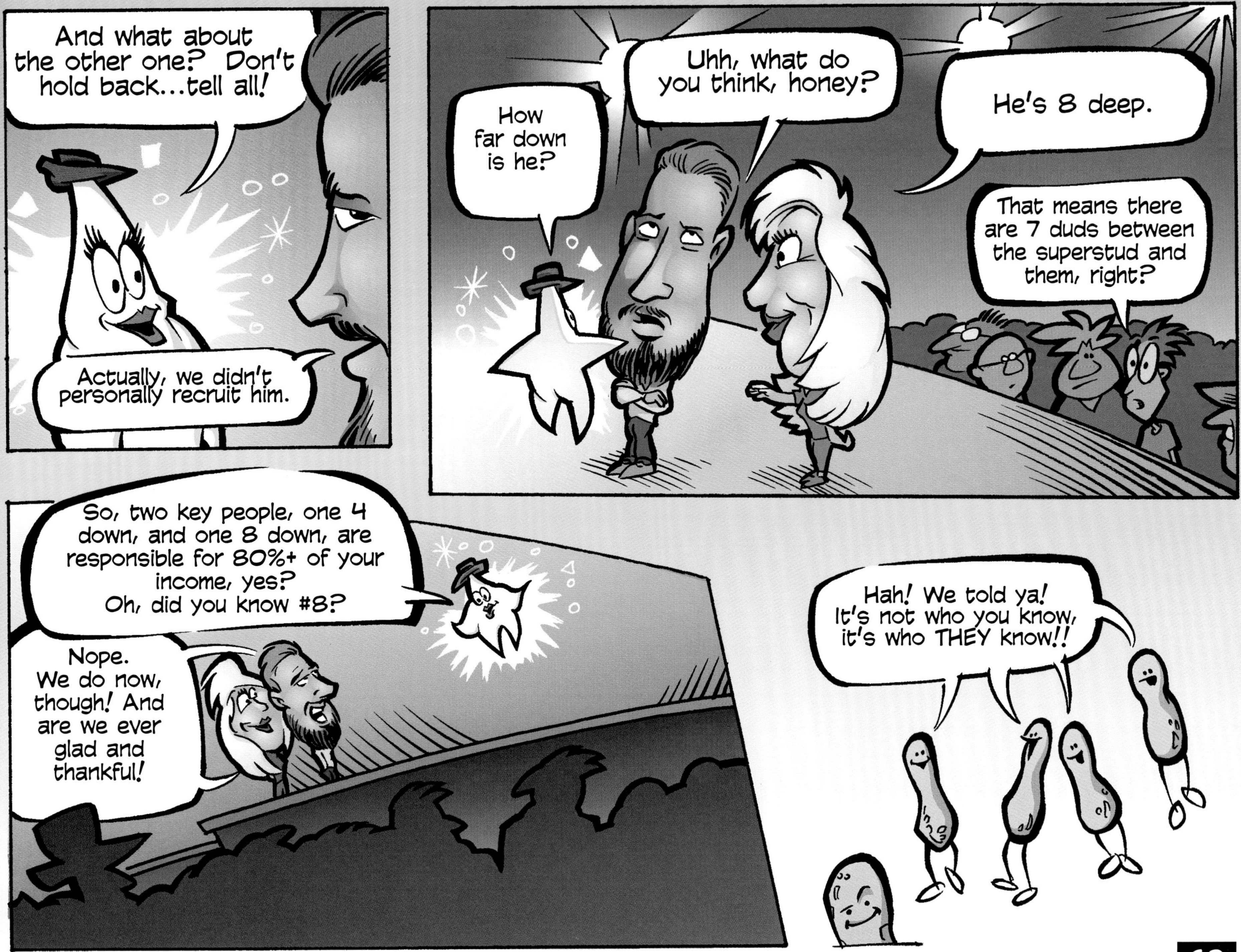
And what about the other one? Don't hold back...tell all!
Actually, we didn't personally recruit him.
How far down is he?
Uhh, what do you think, honey?
He's 8 deep.
That means there are 7 duds between the superstud and them, right?
So, two key people, one 4 down, and one 8 down, are responsible for 80%+ of your income, yes? Oh, did you know #8?
Nope. We do now, though! And are we ever glad and thankful!
Hah! We told ya! It's not who you know, it's who THEY know!!

So how do you spend most of your work time now, or do you still work?
We love the work. I spend my time sponsoring new people and working with them. I have about 6-8 other lines, and I'm constantly showing them how to keep looking for the right ones, and to have those people looking...down down down...because we know the good stuff's often at the bottom.
We travel the country together, telling people our story. We've been in this company 5 years full time, and had never done this before. We're living a dream come true.
Oh--did we tell you that 70 or 80% of our people were never in network marketing before?
Wow!
Gosh!

This is Dave and Connie Johnson. They're in the top 5 earners of another giant company--it has several million independent reps throughout the world... Nu Skin International.
So how many people have you personally sponsored in the 11 years you've been with your company?
About 175.
And how many of them does it take to get most of your income?
One major line, actually. One key person and her organization provides 80% of our income.
One???
How did you meet up?
We met her 12 years ago at a professional meeting...
...and a year later, we brought her into Nu Skin International.

How many of the other front line people are still active?
You know, the usual one in ten if you're lucky. We keep looking for good ones, teaching them to do the same. We're so grateful. And with the new Big Planet program, we'll just get bigger and keep rolling along.

I know can do it! I can do it!! And I wanna flip through decks that have people who have done it before. Gimme those! How do I find those people?
Well, didn't that one couple say 70-80% of theirs hadn't done it before? So I don't wanna skip over those, no way!
Or maybe a good team would do it...or the right product. What if that's what it is?
Yeah! What if that's all it is?
My sister knows somebody who's been doing it for 4 years and still hasn't made any money...so if we go to her, she might be, uhh-
-pukey, right?

And if they get pukey...
Show me the pukeys, show me the pukeys...where are the puk...
Ha ha ha. We're SO GLAD you're going to be coming with us to protect us!!!
Who knows who's going to make it? Or, who might sign up somebody who helps you make it? Can you keep flipping 'till you get to the Aces?
YES already!! Where are they?? Where are they???? I can't STAND IT ANYMORE!!!!
OK ok ok okaaay! Let the hunt begin.

Yeah, ah wanna know how we get TO all dem people don'tchoo?
Ah'm going to people ah DON'T know...muh warm market su--ah mean, it's bad, real bad.
Well, I have some good contacts. I wanna go to them, first.
ESPRESSO
All ya gotta do now is pick yer modus operandi! Yeah!!!!
Modus operandi? What're you, Latin or sumthun? They gotta pick their weapons for the hunt, that's what.
Of course it depends on what they can carry and learn to operate...some are pretty complicated.

Ok, the first step in the dance: Select your methods.
That's all the different ways to reach out to all those who might need it, right?
Remember the mission? Locate the wonderful people from aaawwwl these for whom it's the right thing to be doing...yes?
And within your lifetime, yes?
So therefore, your #1 goal, at the outset, is to spread the story far and wide-
-across the land!!!
Like seeding the earth, right?

-in ways that leave you unscathed. Then see what comes up after your first pass. More might come up on a second or third pass.
And you won't get tangled up with anyone who might sting you, 'cuz I come along, got it?
Hooray for ZAYNO FURST!
So uh, what do we say to all these people?
And how do we get to them all first?
And how do we make them say 'yes'?

We've come a long way from the days of Jesus. They had ONE approach: walk from town to town telling their story. That's how they seeded their piece of the earth. For 3 years they did it together. A good day was any day when they came home at all--alive and in one piece.

Been there, done that. So what else?
The dark side of our world is, instead of spears, the pukeys here just slip us some of that ole' pukey bug--and before you know it-
-we dun got it ourself.
Mmmm. Sounds like a contagious plague.
Then it grows inside us! And then, it's like, well, as if an inner pukey takes over...

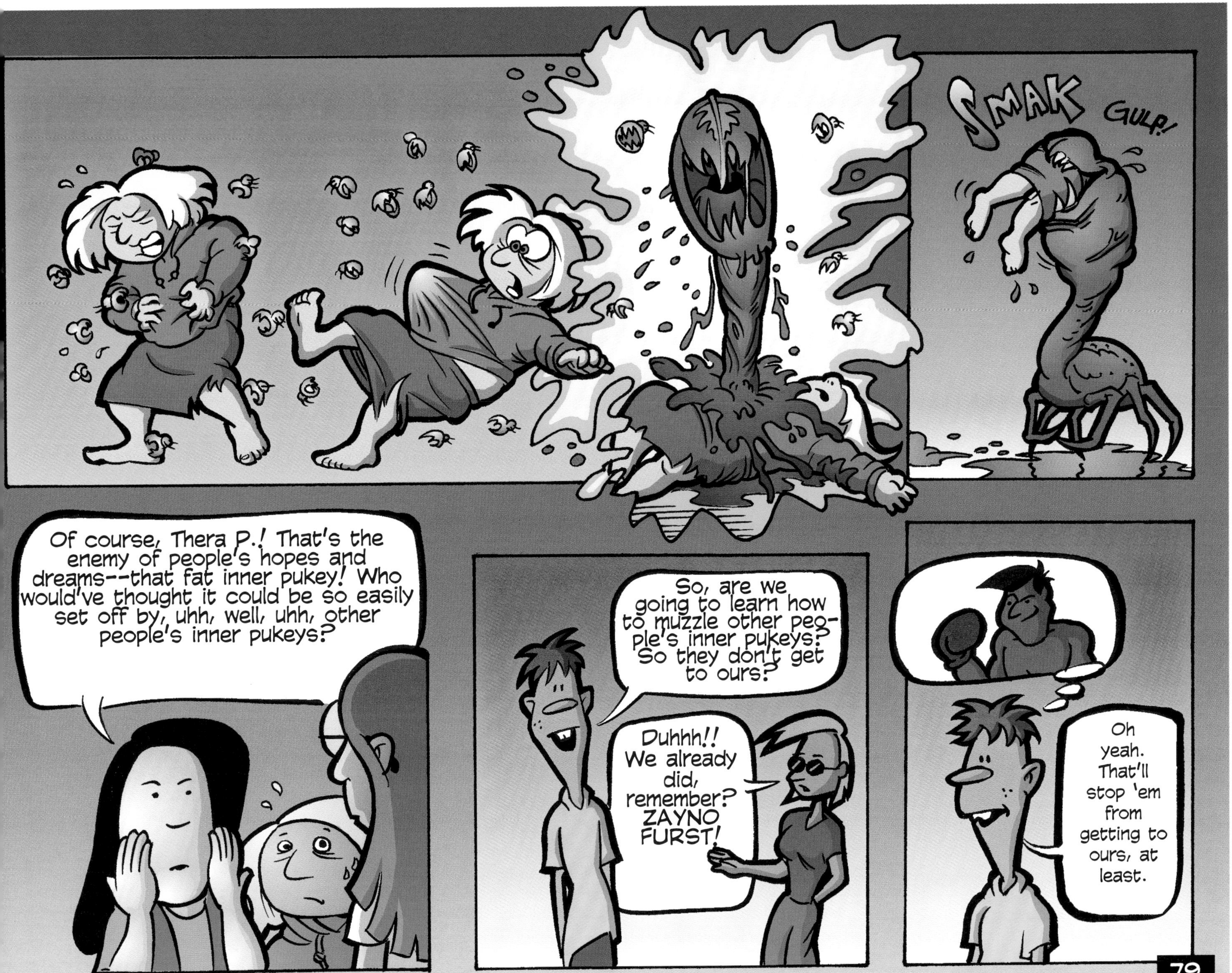
SMAK
GULP!
Of course, Thera P.! That's the enemy of people's hopes and dreams--that fat inner pukey! Who would've thought it could be so easily set off by, uhh, well, uhh, other people's inner pukeys?
So, are we going to learn how to muzzle other peo-ple's inner pukeys? So they don't get to ours?
Duhhh!! We already did, remember? ZAYNO FURST!
Oh yeah. That'll stop 'em from getting to ours, at least.

So the 'first contact' of any reaching out method (ROM) has to be short, but juicy, to attract the Aces. And to hedge your bets, keep 3-5 methods going at all times during the reaching out phase.
3-5? I don't even know 2. So what are they? Where are they?
Let's go shopping. For cool methods-
-of reaching out to the world. To anyone, anywhere, anytime.
Somebody who might even be looking for us, right?
Yeah baby! NOW we're going to be rich!!!

Welcome Super Store shoppers! Everything you see here has helped someone, somewhere, make it...BIG!
Reaching Out Methods
Virtual Super Store
Find the right ones for your business!
That's Ms Stud!, isn't it?
Wow! I never knew there was this much stuff!! I wonder if Mr. Hype knew about all this.
Now we're talkin' So what're the best ones?
All ya gotta do is call everybody you know!

Choosing your favorite methods of reaching out is a lot like buying a car--people gravitate towards different ones.

Here's how to decide what to try first: Check out the goods. See all there is. Then choose. Whatever you gravitate towards are the ones to try first.
Sounds easy enough.

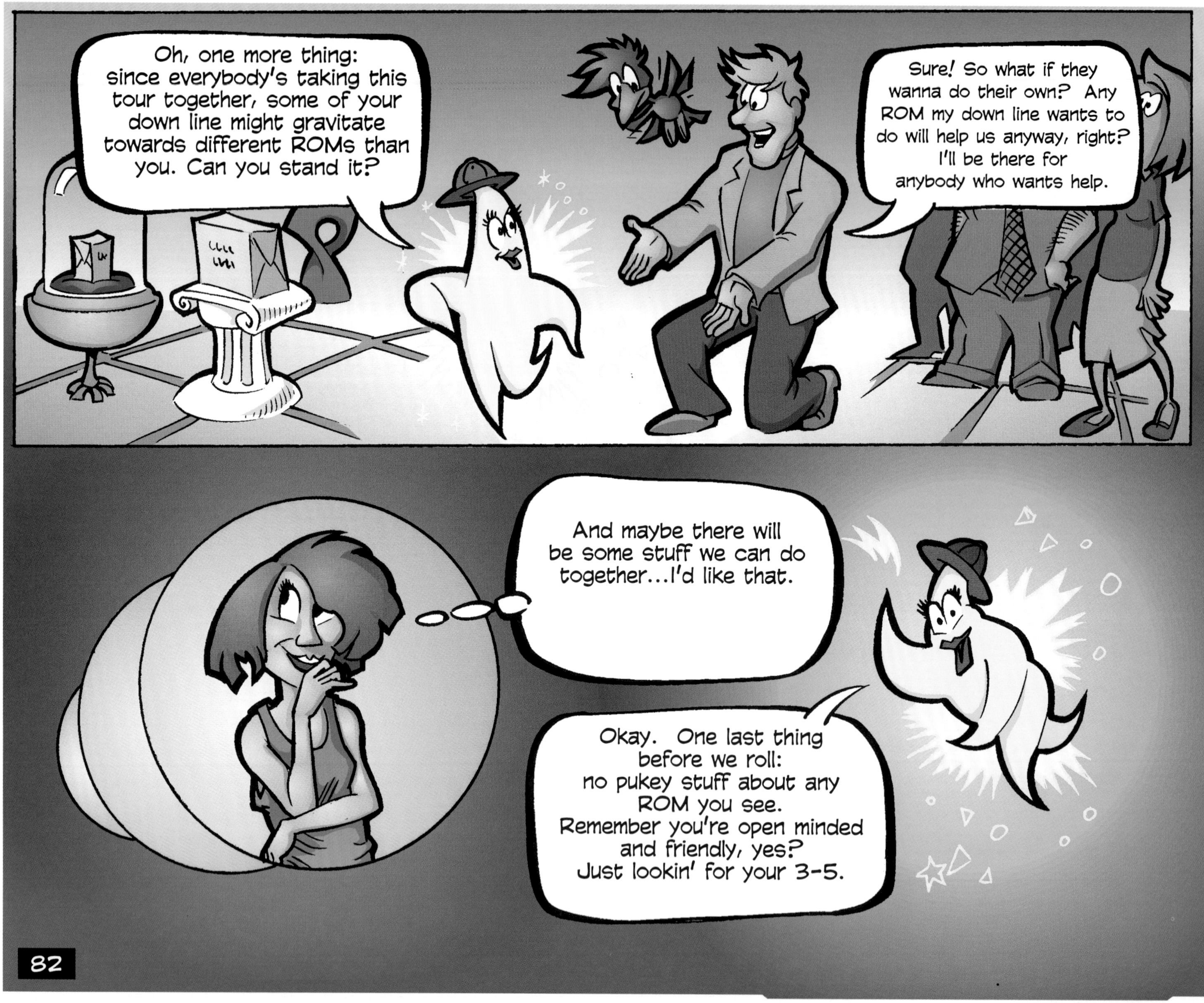
Oh, one more thing: since everybody's taking this tour together, some of your down line might gravitate towards different ROMs than you. Can you stand it?
Sure! So what if they wanna do their own? Any ROM my down line wants to do will help us anyway, right? I'll be there for anybody who wants help.
And maybe there will be some stuff we can do together...I'd like that.
Okay. One last thing before we roll: no pukey stuff about any ROM you see. Remember you're open minded and friendly, yes? Just lookin' for your 3-5.

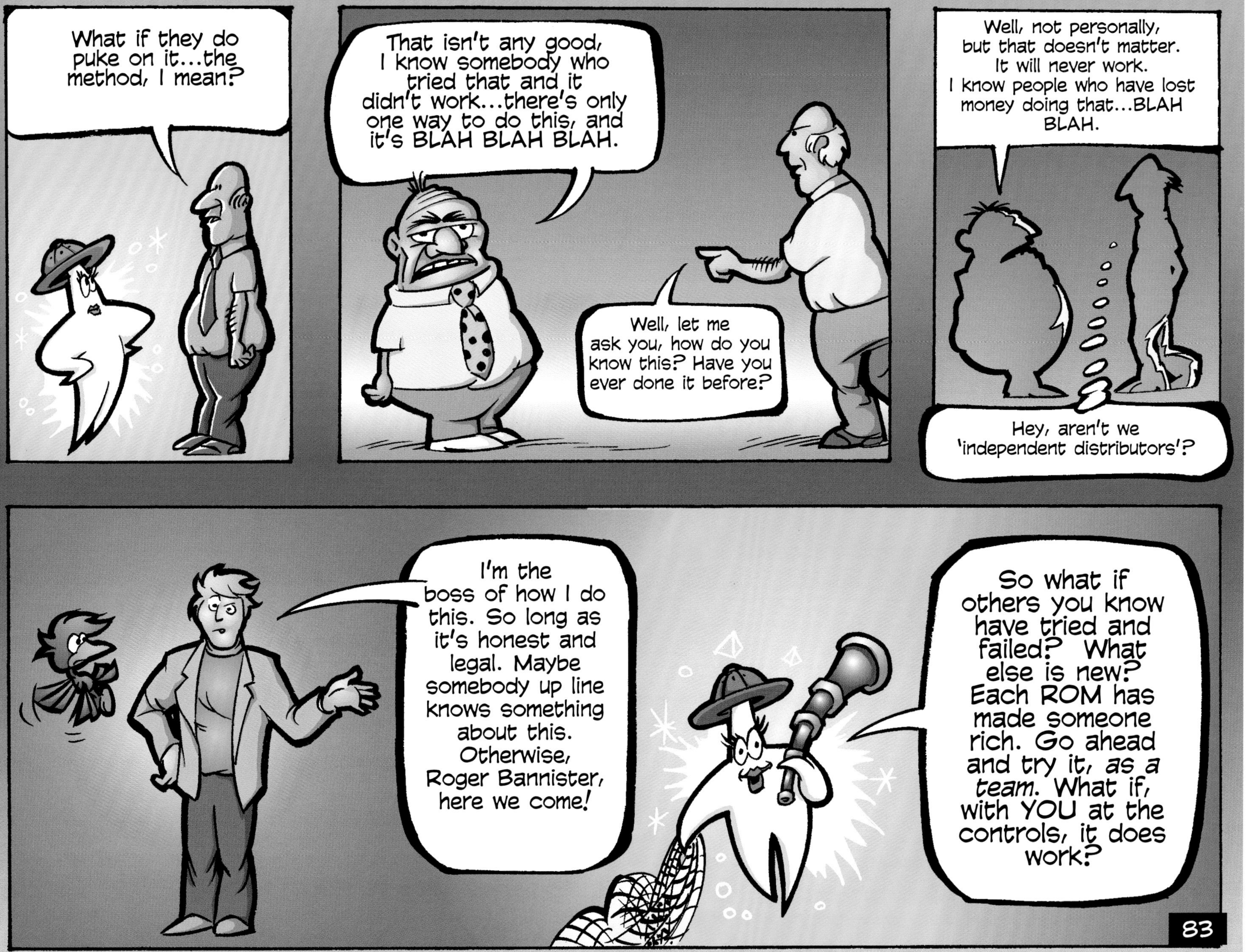
What if they do puke on it...the method, I mean?
That isn't any good, I know somebody who tried that and it didn't work...there's only one way to do this, and it's BLAH BLAH BLAH.
Well, let me ask you, how do you know this? Have you ever done it before?
Well, not personally, but that doesn't matter. It will never work. I know people who have lost money doing that...BLAH BLAH.
Hey, aren't we 'independent distributors'?
I'm the boss of how I do this. So long as it's honest and legal. Maybe somebody up line knows something about this. Otherwise, Roger Bannister, here we come!
So what if others you know have tried and failed? What else is new? Each ROM has made someone rich. Go ahead and try it, *as a team*. What if, with YOU at the controls, it does work?

Who would you take 'how to' advice from? Pick one.
What's your A.Q.?
a. People who act all pukey about it but have never done it before
b. People who have done it once, maybe a few times, but did not succeed
c. Nice people who have never done it before
d. People who have had great to wild success doing it before.
We'd never act pukey!
Totally!
We're trying to get away from the pukeys!!
Well that sounds wonderful, dear. After all, what if it DOES work? That's what I always say about any new idea. And then, I'm always right, no matter what happens.
Why yes... I never thought of that.

ROMs

Reaching Out Methods

to find the ones for whom it's the right thing to be doing

Caution!

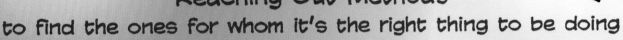

For best results you must be open-minded, friendly and ambitious.
There are no guarantees for success, however PHG*
(*People Have Gotten) results are listed for each method.
These do not consider careless planning, pukey attitudes
or random acts of God.
Samples with underlined text are for you
to fill in with your information. Do that first.

Pick any 3-5...
Let's start with those friends, family and neighbors.
What if we could make 'em come to you?
How'd that be?

Make 'em come to you

Dear friend letter

People you know

PHG*: 1-6%

*people have gotten

Risks!!

Feeling crummy about low response rate

The terrific temptation to follow up

Mary Winner
1111 Stud Lane
Make It City, USA

mo/date/year

Dear (however you normally address them):

Hi! Just a note to let you know that I'm expanding my business, and I was wondering if you could help me.

I'm looking for bright, friendly, and ambitious people who might be looking for some extra income, or, who might be looking for a career change.

Do you know anyone like that?

We market cool/neat/sexy/upscale/health/ communications products/services directly to consumers, like you and me, and the company pays us to find and train others to do the same thing. That's how we expand. We're kind of like reps for them, except we own our own business.

Anyway, do you know anyone who'd like to have more energy, feel younger/ have less expensive communication products/services and wants to make some money with us helping others get the same?

If you know anyone or would like to try the product /service yourself, give me a call at 800.xxx.xxxx and I'll fill you in.

I've used X/done X for X time and have accomplished/experienced X. Before X, I Blah blah. Now, I blah blah. Neat, huh? Anyway, nice thinking of you.

FRIENDLY-signoff
your signature

Your name typed

1. Make a list of 100+ your contacts with addresses
2. Send each a personalized Dear friend letter
3. Send ALL 100+ out at once (within 24-48 hours)
Use classy stationary
Make each letter an original
NO PHOTOCOPIES
Go first class...
1-6% of DFL's typically contact you and express an interest in the product/service or business
Cool. I can do that. An' what about all the ones who didn't respond?
Well, what do you think?! Think you should follow up?
No!!!!!! They might be pukey!!!
You decide...do you want to risk getting the pukey stuff???? Or not?
Izzat all????? One to six of 'em call back?????
OK. So then what? Whadda we say when they call?

Them

Hi! I got your letter, sounds pretty interesting. Tell me more about it.

You

Great! Tell me, what attracted you?

If they say PRODUCT go blue (below).

If they say BUSINESS go green (turn the page).

Them

Blah, blah product.

You

Great! Well, lemme tell you-
our most popular program is/ people with A have really benefitted from: X...

As for me, I started with X.

Before using X, I blah blah

and now I blah blah.

Cool, huh? Would you like to try it and see how it works for you?

Them

How much is it?

You

Well, let me tell you how it comes...

You get XXXXXX and YYYYY...

and they give it to you for $$$$$$...

That's why everybody buys it.

Are you ready to blow your wad and try it?

NO HYPE, e.g. 'it's only'.
That's YOUR opinion...not theirs, yet.

Them

Yeah, I'd like to do/try X.

You

OK, great. Do you have a Master or VISA? You can order direct from the company...and we can do it together...plus, if you want to register, just in case you decide to sell it later, we can do that too. Wanna do that?

Three-way them in to the company 800 #... place their order.

They'll ship it to you direct. I'll give you a call in a week or so to see how its going ,ok?

Thanks! Bye!

Them

Blah, blah more money.

You

Well, let me ask you..have you done any direct sales before? Or any network marketing? Or have you ever owned your own business?

Them

Why yes...blah blah

You

(If you got no specifics, then gently, as if you're talking to a cranky dying relative on his deathbed and someone just now told you he's leaving you his entire fortune...)

Great, what deals/companies have you done??

Them

Blah blah

(from "none-I've only had a job" to listing whatever else they've done.)

Jot down what they say. You may use it later.

You

OK, great. Lemme ask you this: What, ideally, are you looking for?

Listen carefully...are they security/job oriented, or entrepreneurial and looking for a chance to make their own way? Based on what they tell you:

Is this someone for whom your deal looks like the right thing to be doing....????

Them

I'm lookin' for a home based business/$$ for kids education/gangster money. Blah blah.

Check for 'LIFE FORCE'

__lots __so so ____near zero

You

Great! Let me tell you what we're looking for, and we can see if there's a match, ok?

Them

OK

You

We're seeking friendly, ambitious and openminded people who can help us recruit and train our sales force in your area. And, when we find one or two key people we'll help them build a sales force right under them...so they'll be getting overrides and commissions from EVERYBODY's sales in the region. You know, like they do at Merrill Lynch or real estate offices around the country. The top banana gets a piece of everything...What do you think about that? Is that something you could get excited about?

Them

Totally! I could go for that! Blah blah.
How does it work?

You

Let me tell you what we do...I represent a company called X. We market all kinds of cool specialty products... directly to consumers, just like you and me, and we set other people up to do the same thing. That's how our company expands and

that's why they pay us so much.
Think you could do something like that?
-- If we showed you what to do?

Be prepared to take script detours if the prospect throws up a speed bump. Always be ready to say NO first.

Them

You're gonna show me what to do?
I can do that. So whatta ya sellin'?

You

Let me tell you what we market--
upscale nutritionals/telecommunications/ an organic skin care line/energy boosters that don't wipe out your adrenals...
and people can order direct through our catalogues/website/company order line...

Cool, huh?
Of the kinds of products I've mentioned, what interests you the most?

Them

BLah Blah, product.

You

Great! Well, lemme tell you-
our most popular program is/ people with A have really benefitted from: X...
As for me, I started with X. Before using X, I blah blah and now I blah blah.
Cool, huh? Would you like to try it and see how it works for you?

NO COMMENTS ABOUT THE PRICES YET

CAUTION

Them

How much is it?

You

Well, let me tell you how it comes...

You get XXXXXX and YYYYY...

and they give it to you for $$$$$$...

That's why everybody buys it.

Think you'd like to give it a try

before you decide to sell it?

NO HYPE, e.g. 'it's only'. That's YOUR opinion...not theirs, yet.

Them

Yeah, I'd like to do/try X.

You

OK, great. Do you have a Master or VISA? You can order direct from the company...and we can do it together...plus, if you want to register, just in case you decide to sell it later, we can do that too. Wanna do that?

Three-way them in to the company 800 #... place their order.

They'll ship it to you direct. And in the meantime...let me ask you a question-

Them

Ok- tell me what you're doin'.

You

Well, right now we're looking for key people--the ones under whom the rest of the team will be built. But, in scouting out an area, we always come across part-time people as well. And that's great.

So, let me ask you,

how do you see yourself?

As a key person?

Or more of a part-time person?

Them

Oh, I'm a key person (even part-time).

For sure! I'm God's gift...

you'll be able to retire once I get going....

You

Great! So, you're saying you think you could do something like this? If we showed you how?

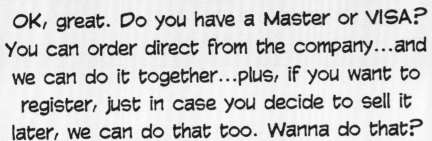

WARNING!!! DANGER HERE!!!!
DO NOT SINK INTO
'TELL-ALL YOU KNOW' TRAP...

Let the tools do the initial qualifying work.
LATER, if they survive the process, you get to help them decide how to get started.

Them

Yeah, babe! Totally! I'm your stud!!!! Tell me all about it!
Yeah I'd like some info on the company and how you get paid.

You

Great. How would you like it?
Do you want to see some printed info, an audio or video?
Would you like to meet some of us, so we can check each other out?
Or would you like to tune in on one of our conference calls so you can see if this is something you can do or not?
I can 3-way you in so it's on my nickel...what's your pleasure?

Them

Blah blah

You

Ok, I'm on it. I'll send the info today/We're getting together x and y/ We have calls x and y. Which time is best for you?
When should I get back to you, so we can see if this is something you should be doing, or not? Great we'll talk then.

So, what happens if we all do this one?
TEAM
Mmmm, well, if 8 people do 100 DFL's = 800 DFL's, yes? PHG = 1-6% with DFL's. So you could get 8-48 NEW PROSPECTS COMIN' TO YOU and to people in your organization. From people they know!!!! Howzat?
1. Have a lick'n stick party chez toi/ anybody's place is great
2. Do everybody's letters on somebody's computer or go to Kinko's and use theirs
3. Everybody signs their letters (use color so readers know it's original), and ads any personal notes (NO HYPE--friendly notes only)*
*optional: Add audio tape/brochure about product/service
4. Mail EVERYBODY's letters at once (24-48 hours)
MAIL
5. Break bread, drink and celebrate together
Lick'n party
Wow!! An' nobody even got puked on!
Uhh, cool. Way cool. I'm doing this one for sure. I can do this...I'm doing this tonite!
That's only one ROM. You and your babies wanna be doing 3-5 ROM's in your first 30-90 days...

WHY???? This sounds like enough to me.
Well, what if they flake on you? I know somebody whose first people all quit. Besides, can't have too many good people, can you?
2-4 GOOD people, plus backups. That's what you want. 'Cuz you're going to help them do these same things, NEXT.
Oh--so we don't do this part forever? Well, isn't that wonderful! OK, I'm ready.
What if...while the letters are on their way, you could be calling a list of people who might be looking for a business to run from home?
Uh, sure, I maybe could do that. Where do ya find those people?
List companies. They compile names, addresses and phone #'s of people who are looking--from health enthusiasts to people looking for home based businesses...
OK, so whadda we do?

You go first

Calling lists

People you don't know

PHG*: 1/2-5%

*people have gotten

Risks!!

Feeling crummy about low response rate

Bigger phone bills

Getting puked out if you do it alone

1. Get a list of 100+ names, addresses and phone #'s of people you're interested in: e.g. bus op or mlm seekers, health enthusiasts, sales professionals, or about any other classification, by type, geographic location, age, sex, WHATEVER you want.

2. Where do we get them?
   See vendor list.

3. What do they cost? Names can range from .20 to $10ea, depending on quantity, quality and how old they are. Pool with your group so you get more for less.

4. Do calling in a space with NO DISTRACTIONS.

5. What's the best time to call? Between 7AM and 9PM THEIR TIME.

Sundays, from 6-9pm are extra productive. People tend to be home, getting ready for Monday. Most evenings (5-6pm & 7:30-9pm) and Saturday mornings are good for catching people at home. Not so good times: Monday eves (sports), and Sunday mornings.
For best results, block out 15 minute segments MINIMUM. (In case they say 'YES'). Get off a quick 3-4 calls during the early AM timeslot before going to work.

6. Go fast. Calling all 100 numbers shouldn't take more than 3 hours total. Call, say 5 at a time. Break a moment or two. Do 5 more. Call them all within a 24 hour period.

(friendly, fuzzyball, non-threatening)

You

Hi. I'm looking for
FIRST & LAST NAME,
is she/he around?

Them

Yeah. That's me!

You

Great. This is FIRST LAST, and
I'm calling you from CITY, STATE.
We're expanding a business
in your area and we're looking for
people to help us.
I understand you might be looking
for a way to make some extra
income from home...
or maybe a lot of income...
Is that true about you?

Them

Yeah...I might be interested...whatcha got?

You

Well, let me ask you..
have you done any direct sales before?
Or any network marketing?
Or have you ever owned your own business?

Them

Why yes...blah blah

Check for 'LIFE FORCE' __lots __so so __near zero

You

(If you got no specifics, then gently, as if you're talking to a cranky dying relative on his deathbed and someone just now told you he's leaving you his entire fortune...)

Great, what deals/companies have you done??

Them

Blah blah

(from "none-I've only had a job" to listing whatever else they've done.)

Jot down what they say. You may use it later.

You

OK, great. Lemme ask you this:
What, ideally, are you looking for?

Listen carefully...are they security/job oriented, or entrepreneurial and looking for a chance to make their own way? Based on what they tell you:

Is this someone for whom your deal looks like the right thing to be doing....????

Them

I'm lookin' for a home based business/$$ for kids education/gangster money. Blah blah.

You

Great! Let me tell you what we're looking for, and we can see if there's a match, ok?

Them

OK

You

We're seeking friendly, ambitious and openminded people who can help us recruit and train our sales force in your area. And, when we find one or two key people we'll help them build a sales force right under them...so they'll be getting overrides and commissions from EVERYBODY's sales in the region. You know, like they do at Merrill Lynch or real estate offices around the country. The top banana gets a piece of everything...What do you think about that? Is that something you could get excited about?

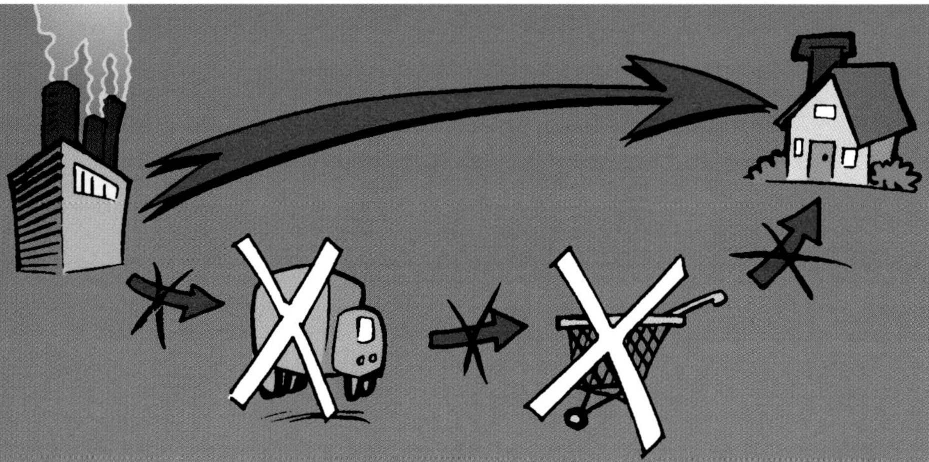

Them

Totally! I could go for that! How does it work?

You

Let me tell you what we do...I represent a company called X. We market all kinds of cool specialty products... directly to consumers, just like you and me, and we set other people up to do the same thing. That's how our company expands and that's why they pay us so much.

Think you could do something like that?

-- If we showed you what to do?

Them

You're gonna show me what to do? I can do that. So whatta ya sellin'?

You

Let me tell you what we market--

<u>upscale nutritionals,</u>
<u>telecommunications,</u>
<u>an organic Skin care line,</u>
<u>energy boosters that don't wipe out your adrenals...</u>

and people can order direct through our <u>catalogues/website/company order line etc.</u>

Cool, huh?

Of the kinds of products I've mentioned, what interests you the most?

Them

BLah Blah, product.

You

Great! Well, lemme tell you-

<u>our most popular program is/ people with A have really benefitted from X...</u>

As for me, I started with <u>X</u>.

Before using <u>X,</u> I <u>blah blah</u> and now I <u>blah blah.</u>

Cool, huh? Would you like to try it and see how it works for you?

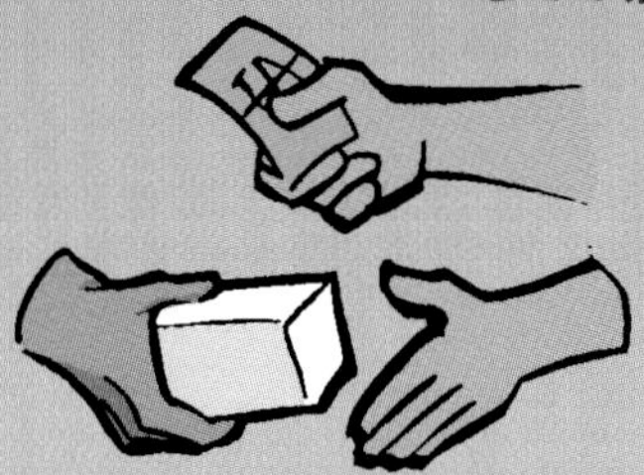

Them

How much is it?

You

Well, let me tell you how it comes...You get <u>XXXXXX and YYYYY...</u> and they give it to you for <u>$$$$$$...</u> That's why everybody buys it. Think you'd like to give it a try before you decide to sell it?

NO HYPE, e.g. 'it's only'. That's YOUR opinion...not theirs, yet.

Them

Yeah, I'd like to do/try X.

You

OK, great. Do you have a Master or VISA? You can order direct from the company...and we can do it together...plus, if you want to register, just in case you decide to sell it later, we can do that too. Wanna do that?

Three-way them in to the company 800 #...place their order.

They'll ship it to you direct. And in the meantime...let me ask you a question-

Them

Ok- so tell me what you're doin'-

You

Well, right now we're looking for key people--the ones under whom the rest of the team will be built. But, in scouting out an area, we always come across part- time people as well. And that's great. So, let me ask you, how do you see yourself? As a key person? Or more of a part-time person?

Them

Oh, I'm a key person/part-time. For sure! I'm God's gift... you'll be able to retire once I get going....blah blah.

You

Great! So, you're saying you think you could do something like this? If we showed you how?

WARNING!!!

Them

Yeah I'd like some info on the company and how you get paid.

You

Great. How would you like it?

Do you want to see some printed info, an audio or video? Would you like to *meet some of us, so we can check each other out? Or would you like to tune in on one of our conference calls so you can see if this is something you can do or not? I can 3-way you in so it's on my nickel..what's your pleasure?

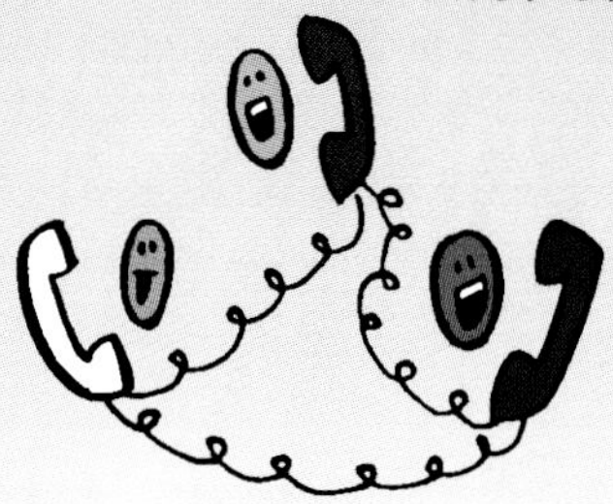

Them

Blah blah

You

Ok, I'm on it. <u>I'll send the info today/We're getting together x and y/we have calls x and y. Which time is best for you?</u> When should I get back to you, so we can see if this is something you should be doing, or not? Great we'll talk then.

*** Get togethers can be professional presentations at business conference centers and University meeting rooms, as well as home parties and bar-b-ques. Remember, this is the first date. Make a good impression.**

TEAM

1. Have calling parties. Get your local team together some place where you can make calls with no distractions. With script in hand, all gather 'round while the bravest one calls someone on their lead list. Others are nearby to hear and follow along, or are on extensions listening in without speaking. (People pick up phone extensions at the first ringing of the prospect's phone, so they're on from the get-go.) No pukey stuff or ridicule if someone tries and it doesn't come off just right...remember your turn is next. Skip speaker phones unless their quality is so high no one at the other end realizes you're using one. Test it first.

Remember, go FIRST CLASS to attract first class.

OR

2. Set up national conference calls where long distance teams can do calls together. (see vendor list for conf. numbers). Everyone has their lead list and their script in front of them. The bravest one starts by three-waying the first name on someone's list--their own or someone else's (presumably downline) on the line. They click back on with the team at the first ring of the prospect's phone, so everyone can hear from the moment the prospect's phone starts to ring. All follow along with the script as the caller takes the prospect through the leading questions.

OR

3. Set up a buddy system for making calls, and do 3-ways if there's just one or two of you working together.

Do these team calls on a regular schedule 1-3x/week.

Note: The teamwork required with list calling creates a mini mastermind and superfun experience for all players. Friendships are created and bonds made that last for years...

If 7 people do 100 calls, that's 700 calls, yes? PHG 1/2%-5% with list calls. So you could get 3-35 new prospects for the business or product for you and your people. Howzat? And some will have experience in direct sales or NM!
Cool...but what if we don't wanna call so many of these guys?

There's a way to make these same people come to you first.

?

Make 'em come to you

Mailing to lists of Opportunity Seekers

People you don't know

PHG*: 1/2-5%

*people have gotten

Risks!!

Getting mad about the wretched low % of response, with possible temporary attitude failure symptoms.

Spending money on the mailers.

PHG 3-20% returned "undeliverable". That's a really big bummer.

1. Get a list of 100+ names, addresses and phone #'s of people you're interested in: e.g. bus op or mlm seekers, health, sports or ANY type of enthusiasts. Ask for them by geographic location, zip, age, sex. WHATEVER you want.

2. Where do we get them?
See vendor list.

LISTS

3. What do they cost?
Names can cost from .20 to $10ea, depending on quality, quantity and how old they are. Pool with your group so you get more for less.

4. Send a letter with audio/brochure or a postcard.

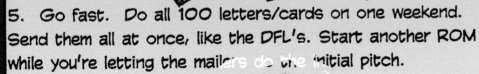

5. Go fast. Do all 100 letters/cards on one weekend. Send them all at once, like the DFL's. Start another ROM while you're letting the mailers do the initial pitch.

6. Look at what you send. Do you want to be perceived as junk mail? Does it look neat and inviting? Will the person receiving it feel special? If not, don't bother. The 1-2% who might have responded to a classy mail piece will just dump it.

FIRST CLASS

Man that's a lot of work for 1-2% return! I mean making it look classy an' all.. ..
Well, this may not be a ROM you should be doing...do others instead...
Well, uhh, what I mean is...
I'm doing this one! I can do a classy mail piece! My babies can use that too! Maybe a stud of the earth type will get my info on my deal from me or one of my babies...
But how do we know?
Duhhhh. I think that's why we're reaching out....Remember that's all you need...the right 1-2%.

Mary Winner
1111 Stud Lane
Make It City, USA

mo/date/year

Dear name from mailing list:

I am writing you because you responded to an ad looking for people interested in a home based business. Is that true about you?

I am expanding in your area, and hope you can help me.

I'm looking for bright, friendly, and ambitious people who might be looking for some extra income, or, who might be looking for a career change.

Do you know anyone like that?

We market cool/neat/sexy/upscale/health/ communications products/services directly to consumers, like you and me. The company pays us to find and train others to do the same thing. That's how we expand. We're kind of like reps for them, except we own our own business.

Anyway, do you know anyone who'd like to have more energy, feel younger/ have less expensive communication products/services and wants to make some money with us helping others get the same?

If you know anyone or would like to try the product /service yourself, give me a call at 800.xxx.xxxx and I'll fill you in.

I've used X/done X for X time and have accomplished/experienced X. Before X, I Blah blah. Now, I blah blah. Neat, huh?

FRIENDLY-signoff
your signature

Your name typed

WANTED: Friendly, open minded, ambitious people who would like to join same. Market cool/sexy/upscale health/communications/hard to find products/services to consumers just like us. Generous pay plan. Team driven. Call 800.xxx.xxxx

So, what happens if we all do this one?
Mmmm, well, if 8 people do 100 mailers = 800 mailers, yes? PHG .25%-2.5% with mailers to opp seekers/special interest groups. Lower than for DFL's. You could have 2-20 NEW PROSPECTS COMIN' TO YOU and people in your organization. Some may have some networking or direct sales experience!! Howzat?
Wow!! An' nobody even got puked on, again!
TEAM
1. Have a lick'n stick party chez toi, anybody's place is great.
2. Do everybody's letters on somebody's computer or go to Kinko's and use theirs.
3. Everybody signs their letters (use color so readers know it's original), and ads any personal notes (NO HYPE--friendly notes only).* *optional. Add audio tape/brochure about product/service
4. Mail EVERYBODY's letters at once
5. Break bread, drink and celebrate together.
Note: Sometimes this is so successful people are willing to pay professional services to send letters for them. A great option for people with some money and not much time.
Uhh, cool. Way cool. There's less response, but probably thousands and thousands of names, right? So we can't run out, right?
So what about these newspaper ads? How do we do these?

What if it does work, hmmm?

First ask up line.

Keep asking up line until you find someone who has successfully run ad campaigns. If your immediate sponsor has no clue, keep asking up line until you find someone who does. Ask whoever has done it **successfully** to show you how, and to help you do the first few. They're usually happy to help, since your success insures their success. Do not let anyone discourage you from trying it.

Make 'em come to you

Newspaper Ads

People you don't know

PHG*: 2-5%

30+ calls from one good Sunday run in a major daily

1-10 calls per ad for smaller papers

*people have gotten

WANTED

Risks!!

Can be expensive

You have to wade through the tire-kickers, and JOB hunters

The temptation to quit too soon

1. Start locally.
(For a national campaign, follow these steps for each region.)

2. Select 1-15 area newspapers
Get copies of the papers you want to run ads in, and review the help wanted and classified sections. Jot down words or phrases that draw your attention. Note how many words per line, and how big the headers are. See how much space your ad would take up, and decide where it might go if you ran yours in that paper. People have been successful with 4-10 line classified ads in both the big dailies (250,000+ circulation) and smaller local dailies and weeklies.
If you don't know the papers you want, visit the local library. Most libraries have a directory of all newspapers, with target audiences, circulations, phone and fax numbers. The librarian can also direct you to nationwide newspaper listing services and publishers.

P.S. While you're at it check out the so called 'penny' papers. You can advertise in dozens of these cheaply, by regions or nationwide. Many people have had great success with product and service results ads in this medium.
E.g. "I lost 18 lbs. with a new, safe product. Ask me how!" 800.xxx.xxxx

Computer literate?
If you know where you want to advertise, try the internet (world wide web, aka www). Most major papers (and cities) have a website. For example, for USA Today, just enter www.usatoday.com (a few end in .net instead of .com) so try both.

Wow that sounds like a lot of work!
Yeah, an' this is just the newspaper ads part!

Uhh, I think we do this stuff in case we have babies who might want to do it, right? So we don't look like doh-dohz when they ask us how...
Ohhhhhhh

Submitting the ad

1. Call the classifieds dept. for the papers you've decided to advertise in.

2. Tell them you want to find out about running a classified ad in the help wanted section. You're advertising a SALES position.

3. Ask how they price ads (usually X$ per line or inch of type).

4. Get the deadline for getting ad copy to them.

5. Get the fax #, the person's name, and ask if you can fax your ad to them. (They're usually delighted; faxes save time and reduce errors).

If they ask: "What kind of position are you advertising?"
Answer: SALES.
(All people you recruit will be selling the product or service, won't they?)

If they ask: "What kind of salary or compensation comes with the position?"
Tell it like it is: "There's no salary. It's a commission position."
There are lots of commission only positions available in papers throughout the U.S.
That's it. Stop talking.

Fax in your neat, clean and final ad copy.

WARNING: DO NOT ATTEMPT TO RECRUIT THE SALESPERSON FROM THE PAPER.
Too many scammers have offended the papers and their staff.
It's not worth the risk.

Make it easy for them to help you

Use the same ad format used by the paper you're faxing to.

Have a teammate review your ad copy before faxing it in.

Type or print your ad so any half wit can read it.

Specify when and where you want the ad run

Include a fax check or credit card # with expiration date, and your signature.

Sample fax to a newspaper's classifieds

Today's date (e.g. January 1, 1999)

Dear NAME OF PAPER classifieds person:

Please run the following ad in the XXXXX section of the classifieds,
DAYS of the week, MONTH & DATE : *(e.g. Sunday and Monday January 1 and 2, 1999)*

Your header here–
Int'l marketing company
expanding on the west coast*
seeking someone with experience
in teaching, public speaking, or who
has owned or operated a business.
**Fax resume to:000-000-00000
or send to P.O. Box X, San Francisco, CA 94111.

**enter the area you are targeting.*
***OR put: Call 1.800.000.0000*

Please charge the ad to my credit card # : XXXXXXXXXXXXXXXX
Expiration: XXXX.

Name on card: ______________________ Signed:______________________________

Pls fax back to confirm this order. Fax #: xxx.xxx.xxxx Thanks!

Bob Jones

800 number and voice mailbox

Get an 800# and voice mailbox
to answer response calls.
Cost is nominal...as little as $5/mo plus per minute charges...which can range from .10-.30 per minute. Lots of plans available.
On any 800# you must have AT LEAST a 45-60 second outgoing message.
Otherwise you cannot record a meaningful message for your callers. The 800# can ring right into the voice mailbox.
When people call, they hear your friendly telemercial, and if they're interested, they'll leave their information.

Sales and marketing

sections of help wanted classifieds pull the most responses. Be prepared to use ZANO FURST for those seeking 9-5 jobs. Others will jump at a real chance to earn a significant income based on personal effort.

Business opportunities

sections pull fewer calls, but callers tend to be looking for opportunities to earn significant incomes, and are often familiar with network marketing. Alternate and see what gets you the best responses.

Recording the telemercial

Read it as many times as it takes until it sounds warm, friendly and inviting.
LISTEN to your own recording before you let others hear it.
Do YOU like it? Would you leave a message? If you think you sound like a total dud, have someone else record the message for you.

Sample Telemercial

Hi! I'm glad you called. No one's here right now, but let me give you some preliminary information.
My name is ABD, and I'm part of an expanding marketing team.
We market cool/neat/sexy/upscale/health/ communications products/services directly to consumers, like you and me. And, we set people up in business all over the country to do the same thing.
Like real estate brokers and security sales companies (like Merrill Lynch), the company we represent pays us overrides on the sales force we recruit and train.
Plus we earn on our own sales.
We're setting up a major sales force in your area, and we need some friendly, openminded and ambitious people to help us. Public speaking and training is a part of the job.
If you think this is something you could do, leave your name, area code and phone #, and a good time to return your call.
We'll call you back in the next day or so-- so we can see if there's a match.
We're especially interested in people who appreciate working with a team of top producers.
And, who are willing to do what it takes to make it big - with us, using a proven system of recruiting and training.
Please spell your name to make sure we get it right. Here comes the beep....

BEEP!

So what should the ad say? What's the best ad?
Who do you want to attract? Business builders? Product buyers?
Remember all the flakes and losers we got last time we ran an ad? I wonder what she'll do about that!

Well I want builders. But also, I'd like people who can benefit from the product, like I have.
The pitch you use in the ad is what does the attracting. Different pitches attract people seeking different things.
Like bait for going fishing? The bait shop has all different kinds of bait.

Let's check out some ads that have run recently, and see what they're asking for.
Dream Opportunity!
We do 100% of the work. No meetings Make big money!
Earn while you sleep!
Turn your computer into a SCREAMING CASH MACHINE!
Overweight?
I lost 22 lbs in 7 weeks, safely.
Leaders wanted
National marketing group expanding in the XXX area. Looking for someone who has owned or operated a business, or has experience in marketing, teaching or public speaking.

Wow! So uh, what ad pulls the most?
Nearly all ads attract someone. Some just pull more than others. And an ad that pulls in one geographic area, may flop in another.
So what's the trick?
OK. First trick-- Ask not: What ad pulls the most? Ask: What's it pulling?
I'm ready...
Whadda ya mean what's it pulling? I'd be grateful for anyone.
Ask two questions of any ad:
1. Who is it attracting? I.e. what might people who respond to this ad expect? What will they have to do to get what's being offered in the ad?
And then--
2. Is that (someone with those expectations) who you want on your team?
Huh?

Let's do one...
Dream Opportunity!
We do 100% of the work. No meetings, no quotas, no training, no phone calls. Make big money! Call NOW 000.000.000
Well, that sounds pretty good to me...where do we sign?

OK, Q-1: What's the person who responds to this expecting?
Well, uh, that there's no work and you can make money.
Is someone with those expectations the one you want on your team? To make money and do no work?

Let's do another one...
Turn $100 into $1,00,000 in 12 months!
AMAZING!
EASY to accomplish.
BRAND NEW!
This program will make you rich! Sit back and wait for the money to come rolling in - and it will!
call 000.000.0000
OK, so what are they selling? And who's it going to attract?
They're selling easy money. Sit back and it'll roll in.
And who will that attract?
People who seek easy money and expect to sit back while it rolls in.
And is that...?
No!
Not who I want on my team.
Who d'you think respond to ads like that?
I dunno. Somebody just like them, I guess...who's looking for fast money with no work.
Maybe it's like those money games. Or an investor type thing.

How about these?
Earn while you sleep! Turn your computer into a SCREAMING CASH MACHINE! It's EASY, FAST, and ANYONE CAN DO IT! Just 1 Hour Per Day pays your car and mortgage payments. Call 000.000.0000
Start earning TODAY! No start up cost! No recruiting! No selling! No telephone calls! and NO time required! Earn HUNDREDS or THOUSANDS a month! It's up to you! Call 000.000.0000

So who are these going to attract?
People who don't expect to do anything to make money, I guess.
I guess I thought saying that stuff would get people...and it did...the wrong ones.
Ask and you shall receive.
They sure sound good, though...don'tcha wish it were true?
Yeah, I know. But does anybody REALLY think you can get good stuff for nothing? Uhh, legally? Honestly??

Maybe that's why that famous person said that famous saying... you know...
What famous saying ?
...Uhh, "There's a sucker born every minute."
Oh.
Yeah.
Ain't it a bummer!! Ah well.
Ok then, so how do I attract the right ones?
Some people have gotten fast matches by writing very specific, focussed ads. They tell about something good that happened to them. For example:
Overweight?
I lost 22 lbs in 7 weeks, safely. Finally!
Call me to find out how!
000.000.0000

So who will this attract?
People who want to lose weight!
Is that who the person running the ad is seeking?
Probably.
Well, yes! Why not?
She can at least sell her product!
And who knows, once people call, maybe she'll ask them if they know someone who might like to earn some extra money by showing others how to do the same thing, right?
Yeah! Hmmm...
Her ad sells results. Her own. Think someone who seeks similar results might at least call on the ad and see what it's about?
Yeah.
I'd like to call it myself.

That's all any ad is expected to do. It's the initial pitch, step one in the dance on the way to finding the right ones...remember?
Did you know that some of the biggest moneymakers in our business have been people who have fallen in love with the product so much that they just couldn't stop talking about it with others?
Like seeing a good movie, right? An tellin' everybody?

People have also gotten results running specific informational ads, if they haven't gotten personal results yet.
AGING REVERSAL
Clinical scientific proof. Medically endorsed. All natural. Wildly profitable.
Call 000.000.0000

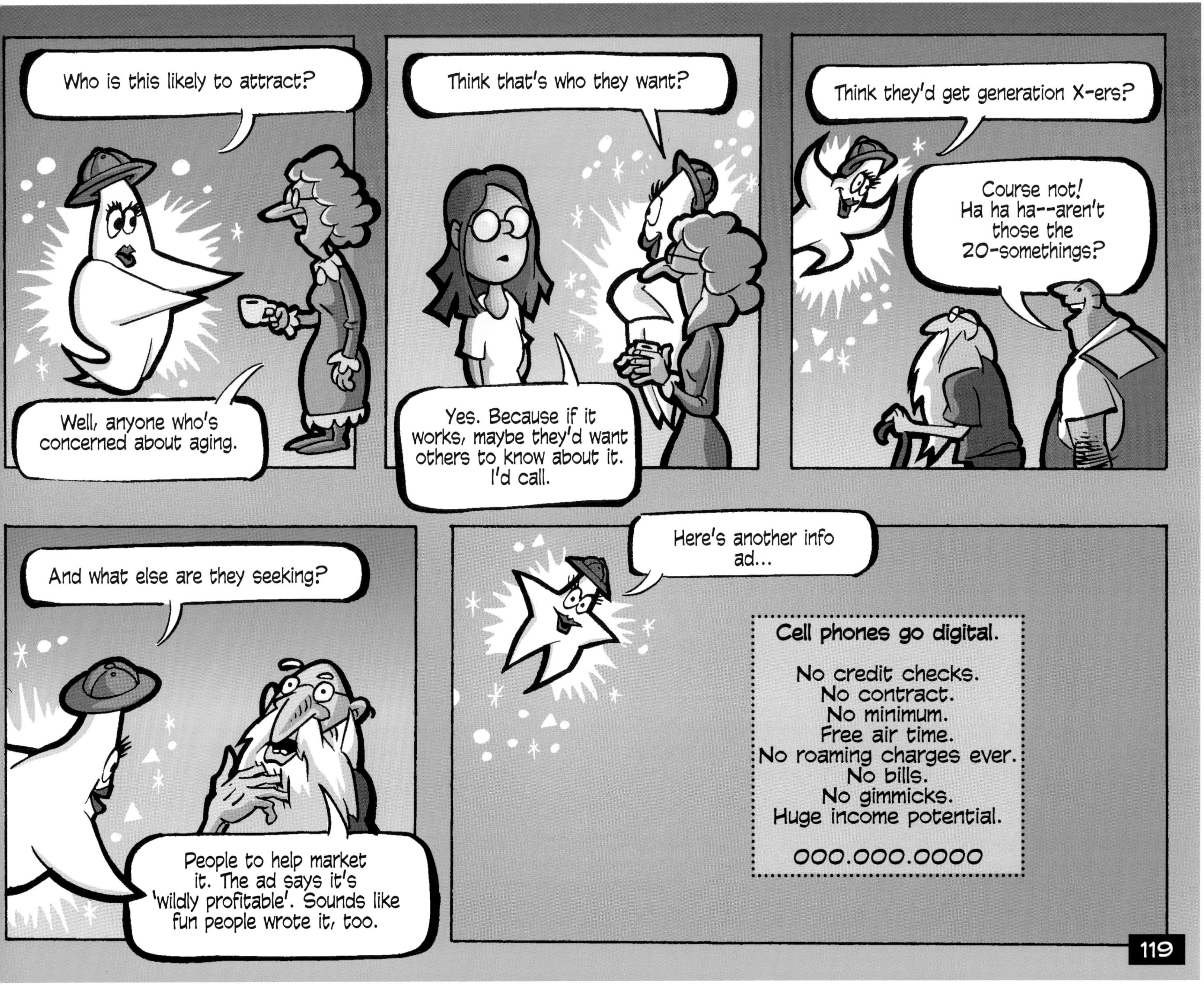
Who is this likely to attract?
Well, anyone who's concerned about aging.
Think that's who they want?
Yes. Because if it works, maybe they'd want others to know about it. I'd call.
Think they'd get generation X-ers?
Course not! Ha ha ha--aren't those the 20-somethings?
And what else are they seeking?
People to help market it. The ad says it's 'wildly profitable'. Sounds like fun people wrote it, too.
Here's another info ad...
Cell phones go digital.
No credit checks.
No contract.
No minimum.
Free air time.
No roaming charges ever.
No bills.
No gimmicks.
Huge income potential.
000.000.0000

That'll attract people looking for phones--that might not have great credit.
Think that's who they're trying to attract?
Sure. People who might be able to buy phones and maybe prepaid time. That's ok, they don't need good credit for that. Maybe they know other people in the same boat.
Yeah. And this might be their chance to start over. A chance to make some good money and have a cell phone, too!
They say that like attracts like. For ads and printed pitches of all kinds, the more focussed the ad is, the easier it is to attract matches.
Well, I want to attract someone who's inner entrepreneur wants to come out--just like me! And uhh, who wants to do something to help the world.
Help the world? Help who in the world do what?
Oh yes... something specific.

Here's another like attracts like ad aimed at professionals:
Leaders wanted
National marketing group expanding in the XXX area. Looking for someone who has owned or operated a business, or has experience in marketing, teaching or public speaking.
Send resume to: Box xxx Anytown USA or call 000.000.0000
Resume? What resume?
People seeking professionals or corporate types often ask for resumes on their first ad in an area. To see who responds.
So who will this attract? What will be the expectations of people who respond?
Uhh, they want people who can train and speak in public.
Think that's who they want?
Totally. How can I get some of them?

People often write ads to attract people like themselves. That's who they're most comfortable with.
Professional types with management and speaking skills might seek out someone like themselves, by asking for those qualifications. And why not? Aren't these useful skills to have in this business?
Yeah! What would you say to those people, I wonder?
Someone else, who has benefitted from a product, might simply seek others who'd like the same fix.
Or if they've gotten cheaper long distance, or better, or less expensive, or more convenient ANYTHING, right?
Right on. If you choose to do ads as one of your 3-5 ROMS, consider ads seeking people who might want the benefit or results that you've gotten from the product or business.
So you can easily talk to ANYONE about what happened to you.
Yeah, I get it! Why stress out inventing future things that haven't happened yet?
Uh, isn't that hype, anyway? The kind we hate to get? Ha!

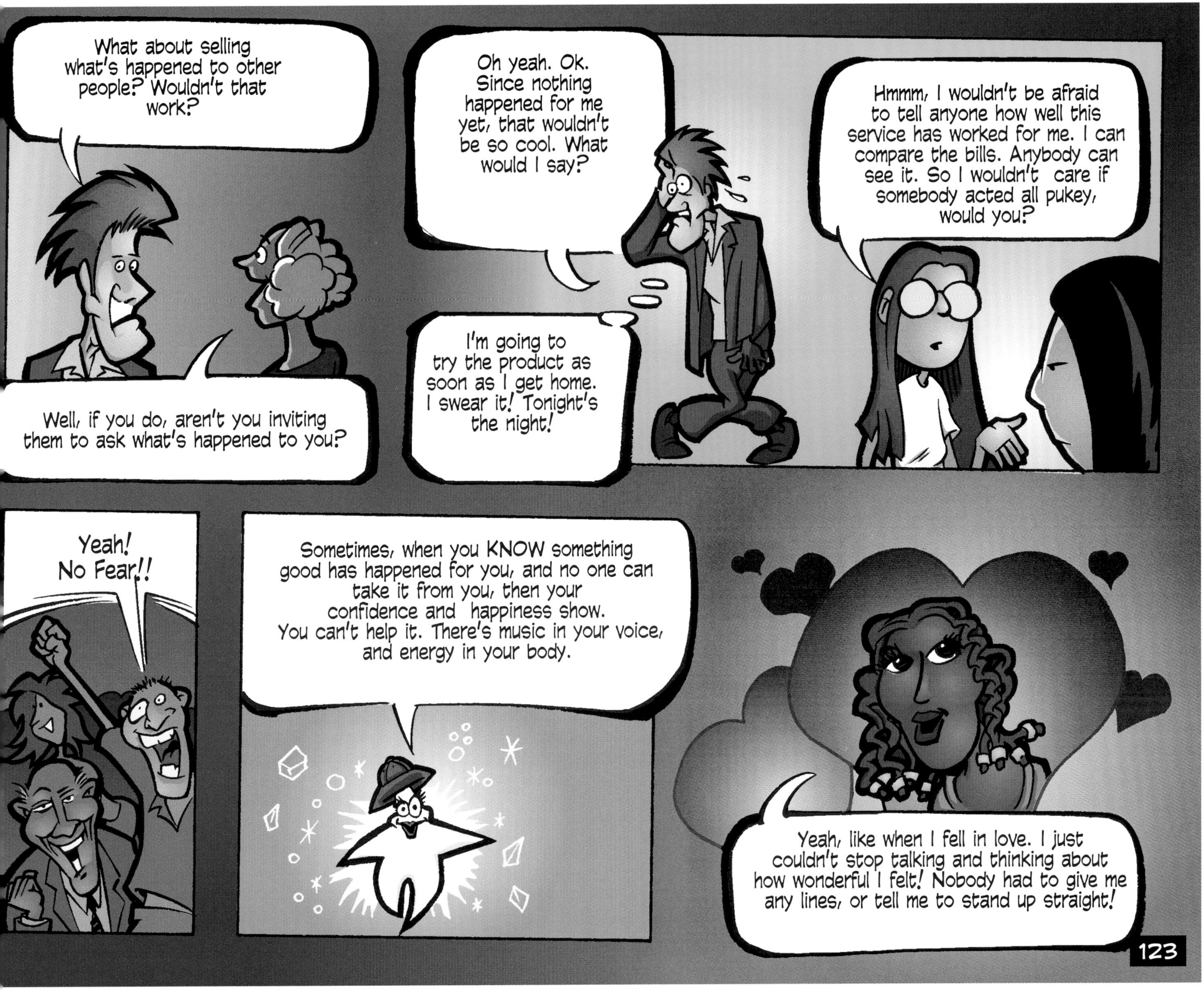
What about selling what's happened to other people? Wouldn't that work?
Well, if you do, aren't you inviting them to ask what's happened to you?
Oh yeah. Ok. Since nothing happened for me yet, that wouldn't be so cool. What would I say?
I'm going to try the product as soon as I get home. I swear it! Tonight's the night!
Hmmm, I wouldn't be afraid to tell anyone how well this service has worked for me. I can compare the bills. Anybody can see it. So I wouldn't care if somebody acted all pukey, would you?
Yeah! No Fear!!
Sometimes, when you KNOW something good has happened for you, and no one can take it from you, then your confidence and happiness show. You can't help it. There's music in your voice, and energy in your body.
Yeah, like when I fell in love. I just couldn't stop talking and thinking about how wonderful I felt! Nobody had to give me any lines, or tell me to stand up straight!

Yeah, and when my own father got his energy back, I was so impressed I told EVERYBODY! I just couldn't help it.
Hmmm--It never even occurred to me to be afraid to tell anyone. I forgot to think of that! Isn't it something! I wonder how that happens.
The good feelings you get from results you experience are like a mirror to the whole world. It comes across as the music in your voice, the energy in your body, and the life force you exude. It's RESULTS ENERGY. And you can't get it unless you get it.
Get what?
Get it.
Results.
YES! Results energy is it! And I know why. It's contagious! Just like those pukey germs.

1. At the beginning of the ad campaign, partners (e.g. team members, upline/downline/sideline, husband and wife, brothers and sisters, friends, etc.), discuss what it's going to take to do it right, and find out who can do what. Some people prefer working the phones, while others are better at preparing first class packages to go out to those who respond to the ads. Other people are great social organizers and enjoy arranging regular pot lucks or other events. (This is the place to invite the new recruits and prospects to meet the rest of the team.) Encourage each person to do what they do the best. So many things need to be done and done well! Try it, improve it...be patient with each other.

Note: Between upline (can be 2 or more) and downline, the upline(s), who might have more money available, can pay a larger share of the ad costs, while the downline do the legwork and get most or all of the leads.

2. Decide what the caller response system will be. Who will take down the names and numbers of callers? How will the leads be distributed?

3. Plan initial 'interview' and presentation schedule and locations (remember: University meeting rooms and business conference centers make a great first impression). Ask the most successful uplines to help conduct the presentations.

4. Plan social events so new prospects can meet the team and each other.

5. Plug new recruits into the reaching out teams immediately!

A SUCCESSFUL DANCE:

Your pitch
(Ad & telemercial)

They want more.
(they leave a message)

1st phone date.
(you call them back)

They pass qualifying phase.
Invite them to an initial 'interview'.

So far so good.
They come to meet the team.

The 'right ones' say YES!

New recruits join reaching out teams.

And newspaper ads are only one ROM. You and your babies wanna be doing 3-5 ROM's in your first 30-90 days...
This one was so long I almost forgot there'd be others. Reaching out sure is a lot of work.
Well, maybe this just isn't something you oughta be doing. it's probably too much for you.
Ok, so where's the millions of people she said could look at our deal right now?
Well, uh, the newspapers should get quite a lot...hmmm...
The major regional and national newspapers give you access to hundreds and thousands of readers who might be looking for more income, or a change in careers. Here's another source that offers people a chance to get the story (pitch) out to hundreds of thousands at once.

They're CARD DECKS. Have you seen them? 30-60 cards in cellophane wrap. Each 'deck' is mailed to tens of thousands of entrepreneurial spirits across the country. Each card describes a different kind of business that can be run from home.
OK!! I wanna do this one!! We've just gotta find some Aces in such a big pile, dontcha think?
Like VAL.Packs or coupon books, right?
Probably costs a small fortune. I wonder how I could ever...
Huh? A card deck? Sounds cool. So uhh, how-

Make 'em come to you

Card Decks

People you don't know

PHG*: 1/4-3% response.

On a 200,000 circ. deck that's 500-6,000 responses.
Of those, 5-10% have been right for the product or business.

Risks!!

Spending money on the decks.

Talking to flaky prospects.

Getting depressed about low response rate.

Most people team up to do decks--they share the costs of the decks, and share the leads...

1. Contact a card deck publisher (see vendor list). Tell them you're considering doing a card in their deck, and ask for a sample deck. You'll see all sorts of business opportunities advertised, from licking envelopes and learning how to be a medical technologist at home to direct sales and network marketing.

2. Publishers mail decks to different people. Opportunity seekers, sales and marketing professionals, health enthusiasts, sports nuts, etc. Some lists are based on census data, like zip codes, or certain income levels, etc. ASK the publishers what 'target audiences' they have so you can tailor your card to attract the ones you want. Ask what cards have pulled well in the past. (Have their decks in front of you so you can ask about specific cards.)

3. Go through the cards in a sample deck and study the ones that you like. As with newpapers ads, jot down phrases and words that attract you.

4. Contact some like advertisers in the deck. Tell them who you are, and that you're thinking about advertising in X deck. Ask how it worked for them? What worked best? Any recommendations?

5. What's the cost? As usual, prices depend on the numbers.
(Numbers = circulation) Cards are 'inserted' into the decks. The larger the circulation of the decks, the less it costs per 'insertion'.
For example, it'll cost you less PER CARD insertion to do a mailing to 200,000, than to 25,000. More is better, and costs less per exposure.

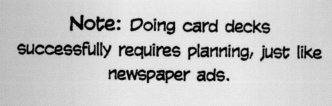

I wanna do those decks with my team...that'll be one of our 3-5! I wannem comin' to me! I like organizing people. I'll get everybody who wants that to do it with me-

Note: Doing card decks successfully requires planning, just like newspaper ads.

Design your card carefully.
Is it a card you would respond to?

Set up an 800#
telemercial with voicemail box.

Set up a response system to handle the inquiries, and have people trained and ready to do follow up.

Be prepared to handle the flaky leads. Qualify them immediately with leading questions, and hang up if you realize they're not the ones you want. Immediately call the next lead.

Do these calls in teams to make the process easier and more fun.

Uhh, way cool. But uhh, think she knows anything that doesn't cost big bucks like this?
I dunno, dude. But if there is, it'll take some imagination, or personality plus, or some kinda effort. I dunno if you got any of that.

Yeah, well, how about you borrow somebody's credit card then.

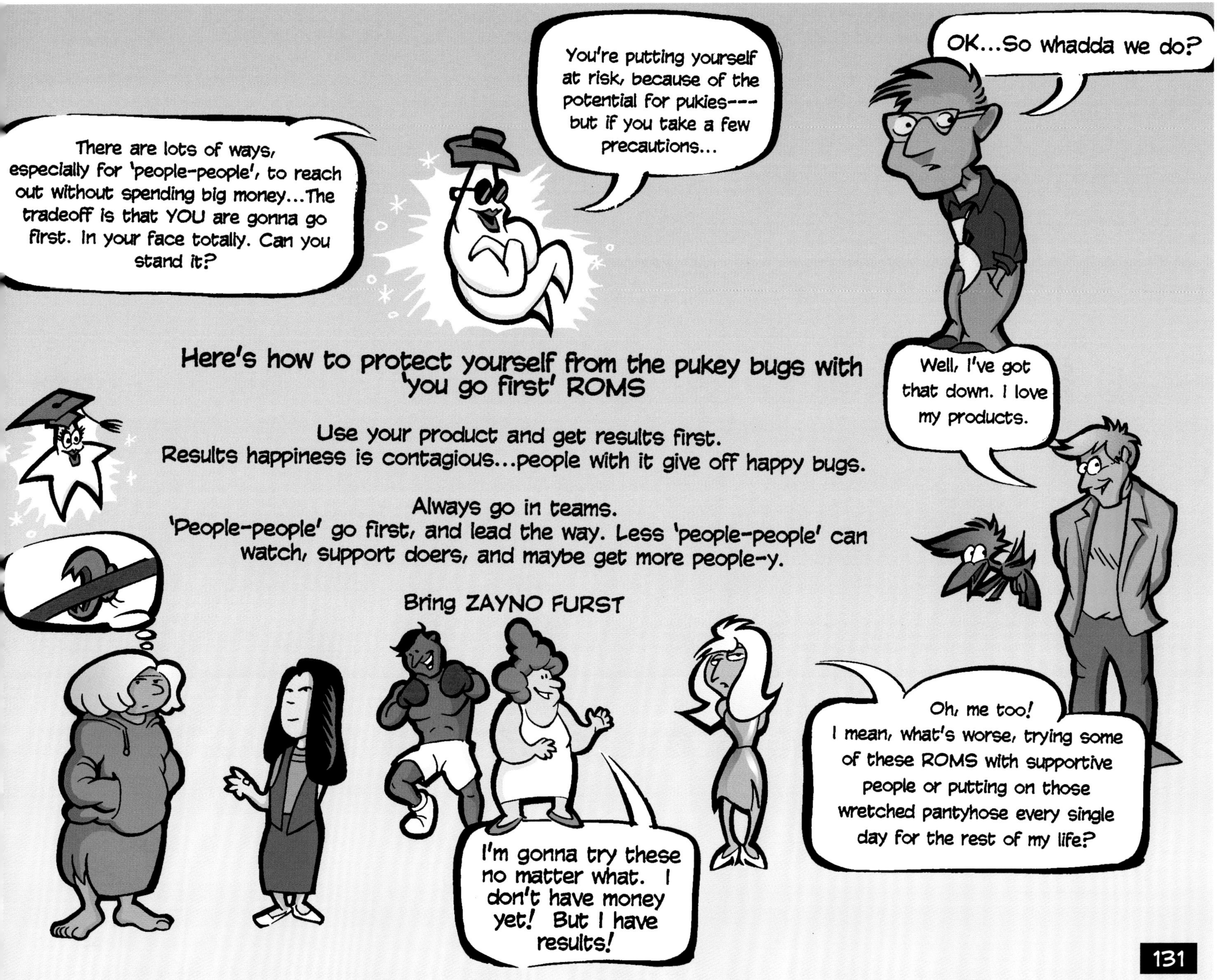
There are lots of ways, especially for 'people-people', to reach out without spending big money...The tradeoff is that YOU are gonna go first. In your face totally. Can you stand it?
You're putting yourself at risk, because of the potential for pukies---but if you take a few precautions...
OK...So whadda we do?
Here's how to protect yourself from the pukey bugs with 'you go first' ROMS
Use your product and get results first.
Results happiness is contagious...people with it give off happy bugs.
Always go in teams.
'People-people' go first, and lead the way. Less 'people-people' can watch, support doers, and maybe get more people-y.
Bring ZAYNO FURST
Well, I've got that down. I love my products.
I'm gonna try these no matter what. I don't have money yet! But I have results!
Oh, me too!
I mean, what's worse, trying some of these ROMS with supportive people or putting on those wretched pantyhose every single day for the rest of my life?

Well, what if it doesn't work? We'll look stupid, right?
Listen, dummy, that's not a lucky question!
Oohh yes, I have the lucky question--what if it does work?
OK, Here are some instant in-your-face things that you can do next week...all tried and true.

You go first

Bump Intos

People you don't know

PHG*: 1/2-5%

*people have gotten

Risks!!

Getting depressed about the pukeys.

The temptation to do it alone.

Spending too much time talking to the wrong ones.

A bump into is an initial baby pitch to see if there's any spark of interest from people you meet as you go about your day. They're quick and friendly.

1. Where? Anywhere and anytime people are brought together for a few moments-- in line at the copy service, the Post Office, a gourmet grocery store, a coffee shop or juice bar. Small indulgence places, like cappuccino or dessert houses, chocolate shoppes, day spas and tennis clubs are extra good. (People always want more of the benefits of these places, if they had the time or the money. And aren't these two things you can help them with?)

2. Who? Choose friendly looking people with good body language. Remember, you're looking for people to partner up with to make your fortune... This is the time to be picky.

Hi. Do you come here a lot?
Blah blah blah
Friendly opener
You live around here?
Blah blah
Check for life force
Great. So, uhh, what do you do?... Cool. So uhh, d'ya love it?
Blah blah...What about you? What do you do?
Wait for them to ask about you...And, if the inevitable is not forthcoming, smile, go back to your book. Keep your eye open for another possibility, if you feel like it. After all, what if the next one's your stud of the earth?
Well, I market all kinds of cool specialty products... directly to consumers, just like you and me, and I show other people how to do the same thing. Do you know anyone who might be looking for some extra income or a career change?
Not that I can think of...
Open the kimono just a little...
Well, if someone pops up onto your screen, here's my card, give me a call, ok? Nice to meet you...a little, anyway!
Sure, yeah, ok.
SMILE. SAY NO MORE. NO STRESS.
Read your book/paper or check out the next person you might want to say hello to. Leave them curious.

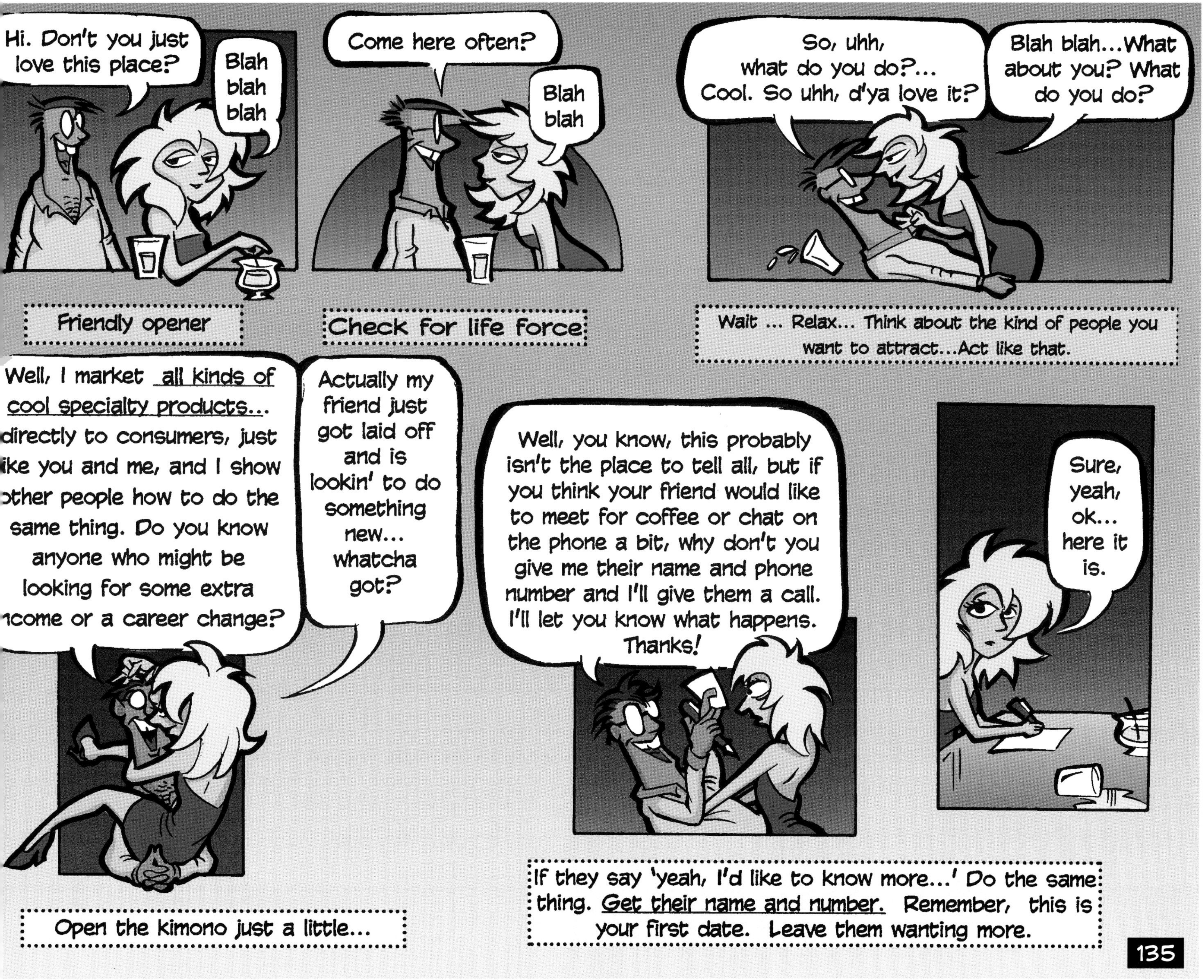

Hi. Don't you just love this place?
Blah blah blah
Friendly opener
Come here often?
Blah blah
Check for life force
So, uhh, what do you do?... Cool. So uhh, d'ya love it?
Blah blah...What about you? What do you do?
Wait ... Relax... Think about the kind of people you want to attract...Act like that.
Well, I market all kinds of cool specialty products... directly to consumers, just ike you and me, and I show ther people how to do the same thing. Do you know anyone who might be looking for some extra ncome or a career change?
Actually my friend just got laid off and is lookin' to do something new... whatcha got?
Open the kimono just a little...
Well, you know, this probably isn't the place to tell all, but if you think your friend would like to meet for coffee or chat on the phone a bit, why don't you give me their name and phone number and I'll give them a call. I'll let you know what happens. Thanks!
Sure, yeah, ok... here it is.
If they say 'yeah, I'd like to know more...' Do the same thing. Get their name and number. Remember, this is your first date. Leave them wanting more.

You go first

Streetwalking

financial districts

People you don't know

PHG*: 1/2-5%

*people have gotten

Risks!!

Wasting time getting up the nerve to do it.

The temptation to do it alone.

Acting too serious.

Talking too much.

Streetwalking is a fast paced, moving, on purpose method of reaching out. The goal is to get as many names and business cards of potential prospects as you can.

Go to areas where there are professional people who might be looking to make a career change, extra income, or simply meet people who have a more attractive lifestyle than the 9-5 routine. To get the best results, go on a regular basis. Get familiar with the foot traffic patterns and the places where the friendliest people hang out.

1. Get 3-10 people together who want to try it or come along and provide moral support.

2. Go to financial districts or an office complex at lunchtime or after work.

3. Get dressed for the people you want to attract.

4. Bring business cards, a small notebook and a pen.

5. The bravest one goes first. Check out the people walking, and select someone who looks friendly, and not self-absorbed. (Keep in mind, you're looking for your partners in fortune...) Walk along side that person, introduce yourself, and explain that you're with a marketing team (point to your pals) expanding in the area and you're looking for bright, friendly, ambitious people who might be looking for a career change or some extra income. Do they know anyone like that? If no, keep moving. If yes, get their name and number. You'll call them in a day or two to see if there might be a match. Keep moving.

6. Cruise the streets for 60-90 minutes. Then, go have a cappuccino, and plan your next ROM.

You go first

Mallcruising

People you don't know

PHG*: 1/2-5%

*people have gotten

Risks!!

Wasting time getting up the nerve to do it.

The temptation to do it alone.

Acting too serious.

Talking too much.

Mallcruising is a slower paced method of reaching out. You are more likely to meet retired people, moms and students looking to make extra income. The goal is to get as many names and business cards of potential prospects as you can.

1. Get 3-10 people together who want to try it or come along and provide moral support.

2. Get dressed for the people you want to attract.

3. Head to the malls or shopping districts any time. Some malls have a 'no soliciting' policy, so make friends with the management or just be inconspicuous.

4. Bring business cards, a small notebook and a pen.

5. Set up a team station in the food court or a nearby coffee shop so team members can meet, go cruising in small teams, regroup and relax. This is a great place to bring new team members to meet the others and practice scripts together. Keep product brochures handy for the curious passerbys.

6. Stay in a team. Look friendly. The bravest one goes first. Check out the people. Pick someone who looks friendly, and not self-absorbed. (Keep in mind, you're looking for your partners in fortune...) Introduce yourself, and explain that you're with a marketing team (point to your pals) expanding in the area and you're looking for bright, friendly, ambitious people who might be looking for a career change or some extra income. Do they know anyone like that? If no, thanks a lot, give them your card, next. If yes, get their name and number. You'll call them in a day or two to see if there might be a match. Keep moving.

You go first

Unemployment offices

People you don't know

PHG*: 1/2-5%

*people have gotten

Risks!!

Talking to deadbeats.

Going to the wrong part of town.

1. Get 3-10 people together who want to try it or come along and provide moral support.

2. Go to the unemployment offices in the upscale areas of town.

3. Get dressed for the people you want to attract.

4. Bring business cards, a small notebook and a pen.

5. Introduce yourselves to the people who work in the office. Tell them you're offering a commission based sales position and can you post flyers, give them your card, or even hold weekly presentations to people who might be interested. If you're friendly, you can develop a great rapport with the counselors on staff.

6. The bravest one goes first. Check out the people and select someone who looks friendly, and not too stressed out. (You're looking for your partners in fortune, yes?) Introduce yourself, and explain that you're with a marketing team (point to your pals) expanding in the area and you're looking for bright, friendly, ambitious people who might be looking for a career change or some extra income. Do they know anyone like that? If no, thanks anyway. If yes, get their name and number. You'll call them in a day or two to see if there might be a match.

Hi! I'm HOT TO TROT and I'm part of a marketing team, and we're out today looking for some friendly ambitious people who might be looking for some extra income, or a maybe career change--you know anyone like that?
Well, uhh, I dunno. What kind of thing is it? It's not one of those things, is it?
Well, uh, it's not-
Ya know, I think our deal is probably not something for you...but have a nice day...
Well, uhhh...ok.
Uhm, I think I could do that...

Yeah, I might know some-one...what's it about?
Uh, cool...Well I don't have time this minute, 'cuz we're on the street today with our marketing team talking to people. So give me your card, or your phone #, and I'll get you some info. Then we can see if this is something you should do, ok?
Oh, and my name's Thera P. And here's my card...nice to meetcha! Gotta go! Talk to you later!

Cool!! Way cool!! What about if we asked 'em for their opinion of our service?
I think you'd need more time to talk then just a few seconds like this...
Yeah, like how about this place? Lemme try it...
Deli
OPEN
Well, lemme tell ya what we're doing...we're introducing a new product that BLAH BLAH BLAH. I've tried it and it works great for me! Before I blah, blah, now I blah, blah... So whadda ya think? Would people around here go for something like that, if it worked for them the way it did for me?
Hi! My name's Hot to Trot, and I'd like to get your reaction to something... you're a savvy local business owner, right?
Well uhh, sure! What is it?
Well, we're introducing this new product line into this area, and I was wondering if you could give me an opinion--if you think it would sell around here, I mean.
TIP
Well, maybe. I know somebody who--uh, how much is it?
Well let me tell ya how it comes.

Wow! Did you see what he just did? Gimme that stuff--I'm trying it too. I want that results energy, too! So I can do that!
Results-energized people become imaginative...have you noticed that? We cook up wild new stuff every day.
Yeah, I heard some people have spoken in front of local clubs and interest groups; an' one did a guest appearance on a local radio show!
If you think up something helpful to offer the audience, people have a reason to come or listen. Some educational tips about a specific aspect of health, communications, or running a business at home.
People in the audience get educated, and some of them have asked the speaker what they recommend, or sell.
I've done that! I had to plan it few weeks in advance though. But I did a little 10 minute presentation at the library on how to get more calcium in your diet without having to drink more milk. It was great fun and I got to give the audience food with good calcium...and then some of them asked if there were any supplements I'd recommend...and I did...of course!
Bookstores, schools, and community centers are great places for such things. Check out your local paper for community events and lectures to get ideas.

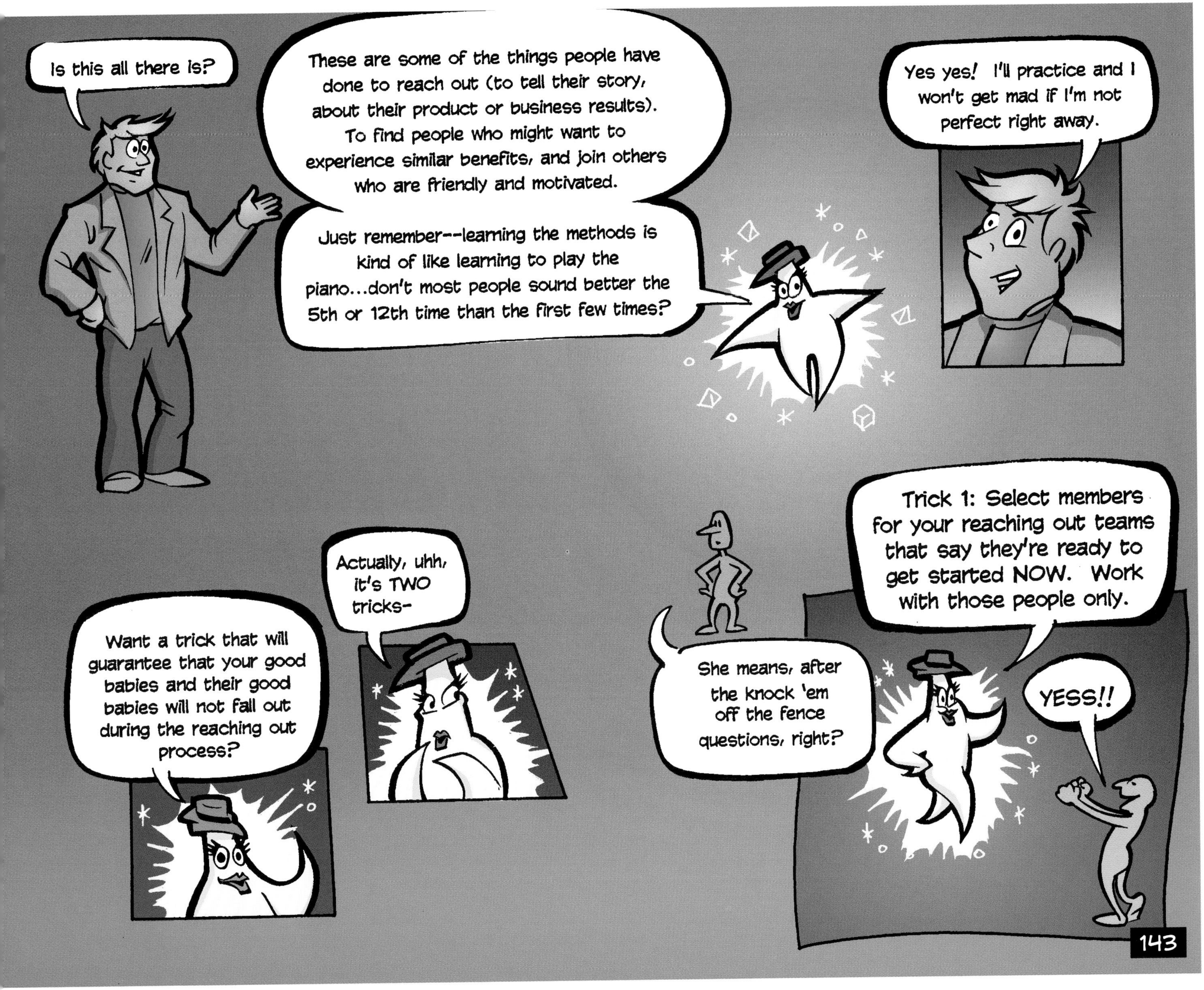
Is this all there is?
These are some of the things people have done to reach out (to tell their story, about their product or business results). To find people who might want to experience similar benefits, and join others who are friendly and motivated.
Just remember--learning the methods is kind of like learning to play the piano...don't most people sound better the 5th or 12th time than the first few times?
Yes yes! I'll practice and I won't get mad if I'm not perfect right away.
Want a trick that will guarantee that your good babies and their good babies will not fall out during the reaching out process?
Actually, uhh, it's TWO tricks-
She means, after the knock 'em off the fence questions, right?
Trick 1: Select members for your reaching out teams that say they're ready to get started NOW. Work with those people only.
YESS!!

Trick 2: Then, within 48 hours of the moment they say NOW, get them to a ROM session or two where a team is actually doing a ROM the new person said they'd like to try. Get them involved in the process immediatley. Help them feel like a part of the team.
So it's AFTER the question, "When are you ready to get started?"
Yeah. But say they already signed the app, decided on the product to buy, and then they say, "Ok, I'm ready to get going. So what do we do now?" Then what should I say?
Then maybe:
How about this? "OK. Here's what we do: you know we reach out and find people who'd like the same kinds of benefits we get, except they just don't know about our stuff yet, right? That's what we're gonna do to grow your business. You got that part, right?"
YES...
"Well, there's lots of ways to reach out to people...whether you know people or not. For example, there's ways to make 'em come to you, and ways where you go first. Ways that cost money and ways that don't. We've got a whole book full. I'll show 'em to you. I got 'em right here.
Then, you tell me which ones you want to try first. Then whatever you want to try, you can watch a team that's doing that thing, either in person or over the phone. Or we'll do it together.
So then, after you watch other people doing it, you can try it. Think you could do that?"
Uh, cool!

And then have the ROM's ready to review with the person. Show them the whole lot, if they want. Do with them what we just did, got it?
As soon as they select 3-5 to try, SET THEM UP ON A TEAM that's doing them, so they can observe others before doing it themselves. Even if you have to be the only other team member.
NEVER LET A NEW BABY do any ROM alone.
Do you want to risk losing them to the pukies, inner or outer?
No! Uh, ok. So how do we set up the teams? Like uh, who goes first?
That's up next. First, review all the methods yourselves, and decide on your 3-5. Meet me in an hour and we'll do the teams...
I'm doin' this one!
That one looks like a lot of work...
Well then, it's prolly not for you...so find another one...
Oh. OK...how about this one...I think I could do this...

I read somewhere that if we bring in one person each month for the next 12 months, and if we help those people do the same thing each month--find one a month for whom it's the right thing to be doing--that at the end of the FIRST 12 months, we'd have over 4,000 people under us! Can you believe that? With these methods, we should be able--
Think that's right? 4,000 people? With ONLY ONE a month each? How could that be? Let's see, month 1 I get 1, or maybe more. Then, month two, I get another one, and my first one gets one...
1 = 2
2 = 4
3 = 8
4 = 16
5 = 32
6 = 64
7 = 128
8 = 256
9 = 512
10 = 1024
11 = 2048
12 = 4096

Wow! If those people just take the product like I am every month, well, they pay us $2.00 per person who does that! That's, uhh, uhh...
We'll be rich! rich! rich!

The Blitz

4-6 weeks in advance leaders get the teams together, by geographic area. Set the strike date.

Decide what ROMs you'll do, and who will be on what teams.
Plan at least 5+ methods at once.
(For example; ads, DFLs, streetwalking, mallcruising, unemployment offices, mailing/calling to lists.)
Practice scripts, plan walking routes, buy names, plan ads, etc.
Schedule presentation times and locations.

Make a calendar for each week of the blitz...
To cover an area, plan 30-90 days.

Every 30 days new team members take the baton. Relay, so no one group tires out.

Could you tell us, with all these methods of reaching out, what would you do-if you wanted to go REALLY fast?
The blitz. A total blitz. Then a few Palm days. Repeat as necessary.

WARNING!
Before you plan a blitz, have a stud upline or two comitted to helping you.

Aha! That means maybe the next month we can do it again-but with our new people doing some of what we do now-and with them getting all the next batches of new people, right?
When you blanket a geographic area with 5+ ROMs, at once, that is a Blitz.
Yeah, and then maybe we'd be the big guns--
At least mid size-
Wow!!
Yeah! What if I get an avalanche of leads? Some of them could be top banana material.
Your stud upline should be on call by phone, for conducting live dog 'n pony shows, and for personal interviews with classy prospects.
Think those big guys would come for us?
If top producers (above you) know you are planning a major hit like the Blitz, they will be available. We're talking top bananas, not weenies. Try it.
Set it up and they will come.
Yeah, my stud upline says to let the telemercials, 24 hour calls, mailers or other initial pitch forms do the screening. Or me, if I take the calls.
Then, if they're really interested, she'll step right up.
Well that sounds reasonable, don'tcha think?
Cool!!!!!!! So, uh, like which ones would we do in a Blitz?

2 Sample Blitz Weeks

Sunday	Monday	Tuesday	Wednesday	Thursday	Friday	Saturday
Local Ads Hit	Practice Scripts with team	Unemployment office with team	team Calls	DFLs	Street-Walking with team	BBQ party with Prospects and team

Sunday	Monday	Tuesday	Wednesday	Thursday	Friday	Saturday
More ads hit	Mall Cruising with team	Bump-intos	team Calls	College placement centers	Happy hour with team study Scripts	Super Saturday Bus Op & Training

"Take care of your health and avoid stress, consolidate your energy and build up your strength."

Sun Tzu
The Art of War
p.153.

Ok, so now, uhh, do we just, like DO it? Just like that?

Keeping it together

COME ON IN!
ADS
BUMP INTOS
DEAR FRIEND LETTERS
STREET-WALKING

Want to see how they do this one? You can listen in on their call and see how they do it. They're just getting started.
TEAM CONF CALLING
This is good. I'm not quite ready.
Yeah. I just want to see this one and then I'll be ready.
OK. Who feels the bravest today and gets to go first?
Me! I'll go first!

OK, does everyone have their scripts in front of them?
Everyone have ZAYNO FURST?
YES!!
OK, let's roll. Everybody mute your phones while Mary three ways out the first name on her list. Remember Mary, AS SOON AS THEIR PHONE STARTS TO RING, click us all back in, ok? So we can hear everything from the moment they pick up their phone.
OK!
All mute your phones, and tune in...she'll be right back--
Hello?
Hi. I'm looking for Joe Cool. Is he around?
Yeah!. That's me...
Great! This is Mary Super and I'm calling you becuz I understand you're looking to make some extra income from home...or maybe some obscene income...is that true about you? You lookin' to make some extra money from home?
Yeah, I am, actually...

Great! What, ideally, are you looking for?
Actually, I heard about something where you only hafta lick and stamp envelopes. I could do that, I think. You got somethin' like that? 'Cuz I can't sell...
Oh, I see. Well shucks, ya know Joe, I think our business is prolly not something for you. At least not now. I'm sure you'll find something just right, though. Have a great day, ok? Another call! Gotta go! See ya! Bye!
OK. Next call. Did everybody get that? Remember what we're looking for? People for whom our business is the right thing to be doing NOW! Do you wanna recruit people ya hafta drag across the finish line? Yes or no? You can always start a list of 'CALL LATERS.' For now, don't you want it in your lifetime? YES????
Good Job!
Way to go!!
Yes!!! Totally!!

I coulda sold 'im, I bet! I coulda had 'im!
Yeah, me too.
Yeah, but so what if ya got him? How fast d'you think he'd go? I'm sick a' draggin' people. I want a top gun. NOW. An lookit all those names they still gotta call--what if it's one of them?
Well, uh, hmmm. I guess-uhh, hmm.
Do you really want everyone you could get?
OK, Who wants to go next?
Me! I wanna try it.
OK. You got the script?
I've got it right here! And I've been practicing.

I'm not doin' this in front of nobody. I can do it myself.
Yeah, me too. I don't want 'em lookin' at me...I don't need 'em.
Got your list? Show 'em what you can do!
I'm ready...lemme hit my FLASH button
Hello?
Hi! I'm lookin' for May Stud, is she in?
Sure, who shall I say is calling?
Tell her it's Hot to Trot from San Francisco, and that I'm getting back to her about a business we're expanding out in your area.
Oh, yeah? What kind of business?
Well, uh, maybe she'll let you listen in on the extension or speakerphone...I should talk to her first, though, if you know what I mean...

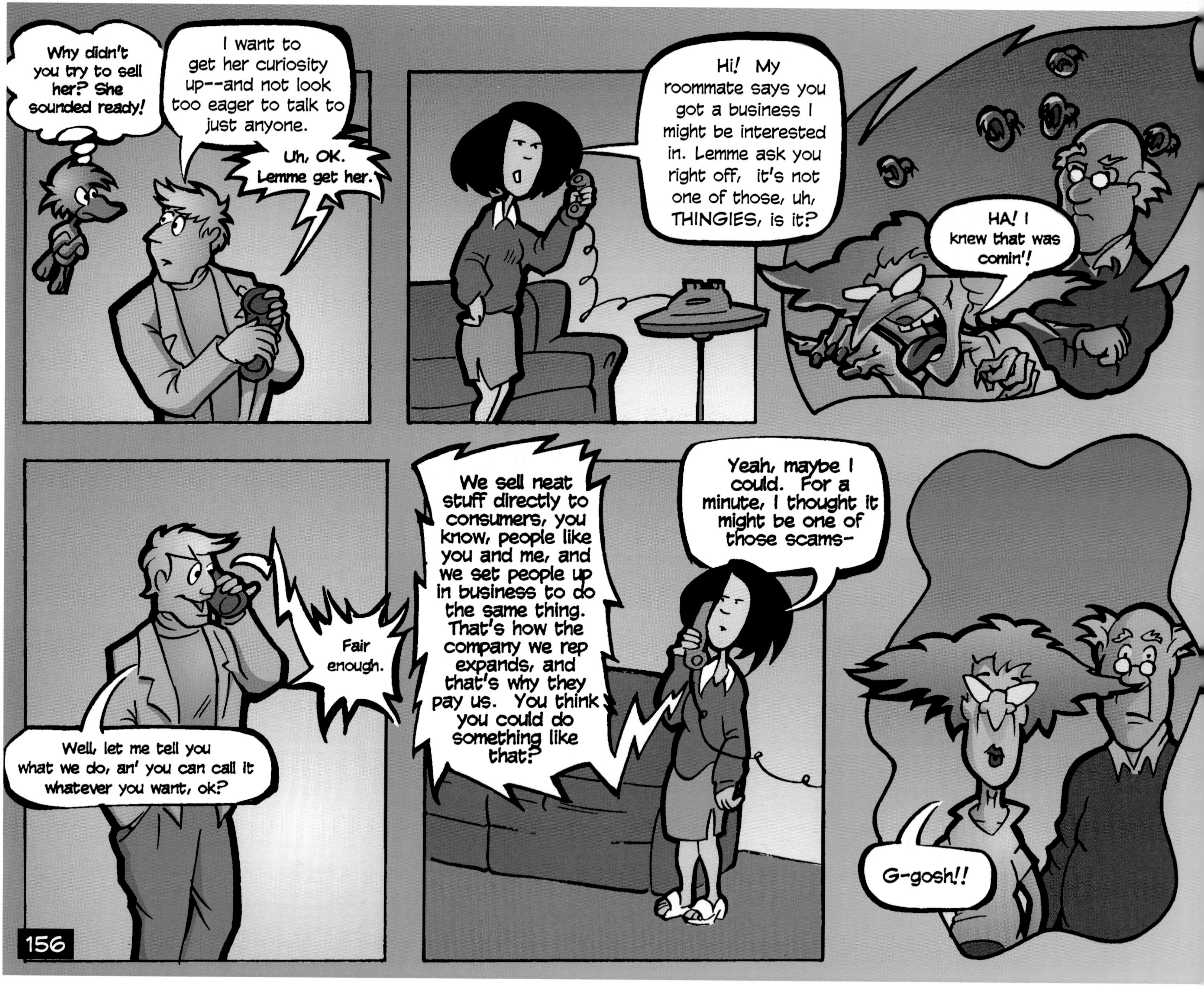
Why didn't you try to sell her? She sounded ready!
I want to get her curiosity up--and not look too eager to talk to just anyone.
Uh, OK. Lemme get her.
Hi! My roommate says you got a business I might be interested in. Lemme ask you right off, it's not one of those, uh, THINGIES, is it?
HA! I knew that was comin'!
Well, let me tell you what we do, an' you can call it whatever you want, ok?
Fair enough.
We sell neat stuff directly to consumers, you know, people like you and me, and we set people up in business to do the same thing. That's how the company we rep expands, and that's why they pay us. You think you could do something like that?
Yeah, maybe I could. For a minute, I thought it might be one of those scams-
G-gosh!!

Yeah, I know what you mean. Well, let me ask you-what, ideally are you looking for? I understand you're looking to make some money from home--maybe even obscene money, huh? Is that true about you?
Yes...I'm looking to supplement my income, because I can't seem to make ends meet. An extra $400 or so a month would be wonderful. Although obscene income sounds pretty good--ha ha. My roommate's in the same boat, got room for two?
Maybe, just maybe. Lemme ask you, have you ever done any direct sales before, or network marketing, or have you ever owned your own business?
Yuck yuck! Did you see him ALMOST get it? Ha! Well, I guess if he could get it, it can't be us, huh?
Yeah, we just gotta know the words to say. And if they're really, uh, unbearable and pukey, we'll give 'em a piece of our mind and hang up. They can just stay the way they are.
Say, what if our new babies could watch first, just like this, and see the top enchiladas getting it? The pukies and them, I mean. Then at least they'd know it wasn't them...
And then when they try it with a supportive, friendly team like us, well, maybe they wouldn't crash...I mean how could they when we're all glued together?

Remember your mission: Find ones for whom this is the right thing to be doing. Yes? And the trick to it is surviving the process of wading through ALL the wrong ones...and you know how many that is, right?
Yes!!!
She means 'temporarily' wrong ones, right?
I don't wanna be a wet blanket, but it's gonna be a lot of work to set all that up, don'tcha think? I mean, what if they flake any-way? Aren't most people gonna flake, anyway?
Let's say doing ROMs in teams helps just 2 or 3 of your people survive the trip and bloom. Is it worth it, even if the rest still flake? Remember, how many good people do you need to make major money?
2-4. Most biggies have done it with 2-4 really good people...that's what we found out...
So, is it worth it???
Well, I'll try it, but it better work!
Let's get back to Hot...

Well, sounds very interesting. And I'd like to try the product. But I want to know, how do we actually do this? I mean without dealing with friends, family and neighbors?
Yes. So how does it happen, exactly? Without you know who at first?
Ok, here's what we do. You know we reach out and find people who'd like to get the same kinds of benefits we get, except they just don't know about us yet, right? You got that concept, right?
There are lots of ways. There're ways where you can make people come to you, and ways where you go first. People you know and people you don't know. I'll show them to you and then you can pick any 3-5 you want.
Plus, we do it all in teams because it's easier and more fun.
Teams? What teams?
Well, for example, this call with you is one of our training calls, and we have some friendly people who'd like to say 'hi' to you...what do you think of that?
Really? Gosh! Yes!
OK guys...say hello to May Stud!
Hi, MAY STUD!!!!!!
Hi MAY! When I first started doing this, I felt the same way about going to people I know. Then I found things like this, that are much more fun. And after I got the business going with a few people, some of my friends came to me to ask what I was doing. I LOVED it!

Gosh, sounds wonderful. Hmm. Ok, I just have one question right now...uh, how much will I have to invest? What's it gonna cost?
Well, that depends. How fast do you want to go? Turbo speed, medium or the leisure track?
We can do this with money or imagination. Whatever you've got the most of. Along with some life force and good energy. You just tell me how fast.
Well, I'd like to go as fast as I can. I probably have more imagination than money at this point, but I know people that might help me. I guess that's my imagination kicking in, huh?
Yup. So, let me ask you this: How much time can you commit to the business?
Well, prolly 7-10 hours a week to start...more if it goes well.
Great! And how much of a budget can you commit to building your business?
Budget?
Yeah. You know, for business cards and maybe some ads. Pick a number between $50 and $500 per month. Tell me what you can do so I can help you get the most bang for your buck--and your time, too.
Well, how about $150 per month.
Great. We can work with that. Now, when are you ready to get started?

Umm, next week. Let's see, I could do Tuesday, say 6-8pm. OK by you?
I'm on. It's in my calendar. You too?
Got it. Now, you said that if I do this with you, I'd be on teams like this too? Doing lots of different things to find people for my team?
Yes. As soon as you're registered with the company, and you get on the product we'll review the reaching out methods together right off. You can pick your 3-5. Then we'll get you on the ROM teams pronto.
Great. So how much is the product?
Well, let me tell you how it comes, ok? You get BLAH BLAH. And for that, it's $. And of course, that's why everybody buys it. Isn't that neat? So which one do you want to do? Package A, B or C?
B sounds good. Think I'll do that.
OK, I'll call us in to the company right now, so we can get you registered, order your product. You have a VISA or Master or one of those?
Let me fish it out...
Ok, I'm gonna put you on hold while I 3-way us in. Don't hang up, ok? I'll be right back.

You all know what this means, right?
Yeah! We're gonna be rich rich rich!
Hot's done step 1 in the dance. Even step 2. His person'll get on the product or service, and hopefully, experience the benefits of the product she's going to be selling.
Then, she'll pick her 3-5 ROMs, and hop onto a few ROM teams immediately...so reaching out starts instantly and painlessly.
1
2
ROM
ROM
ROM
ROM
And all this within 48 hours of the 'yes' word from her. Everybody got that?
...and then we preserve her attitude, in case of pukies or forever maybes, yes?
So uh, what if she doesn't know much about the product or company--will it be good for her to start actually talking to people so soon?
Did you notice that new babies are not 'talking to' people?
They're not?
They're ASKING QUESTIONS. The Leading Questions. All of which are written down in The Truth book in front of them. Just add a little life force.
Ahh yes! Of course!

So when will they learn the nitty gritty?
During the time they're not on team conference calls, or not doing DFL's and such, they can be joining small study groups, live, phone or web seminars, or do self-study time with company literature about the product benefits, pricing, and comp plan.
OK. But what if somebody has technical questions on these calls?
Remember your mission, hmmm? In your lifetime? Therefore: Direct people to the information resources your company has so 'technical information seekers' can do whatever 'due diligence' they want to do, before you have any further conversation.
All class A companies make technical, corporate, pay plan etc., information available-24-hour conference calls, brochures, seminars, fax on demands, etc. Cool people will appreciate that.
Yeah, why get your underwear all up in a bunch about somebody who hasn't even tried it yet?
Yeah. Right. Until people try the product, they'll never have results. They'll just have to try it, that's all.
Your mission is to relate results and see who else might want them. Companies agree. That's why they prepare the technical, corporate and comp plan info.Then they recruit distributors to do the reaching out to tell results and build a sales force.
So use them for their strengths, while they use you for yours.
Yeah, we do have a big fat binder with lots of that stuff in it...plus audios, videos, an' everything.
She says just add those stuck folks to a 'later' list and keep reaching out for those who will help you get there now.

OK. Well, at least that's people in the pipeline. So that's good, right? I mean they might still be possibles...
I'm confused. So what does 'right' mean then, exactly? Just about everyone I know needs the benefits we offer...I just know our stuff'd help them...so I WANT them to have it and do it. So, is she saying they might not be 'right'?
A 'right' one refers to someones mental state.
Heavy--
A 'right one' is in a state of readiness. As in, 'able to respond without delay or hesitation', (per Webster's). That's ready.
Ready for what?
'Right' ones are ready to make a change. They're ready to to try something new and different that could bring benefits they want right now.
Ahhh. I thought "right" meant they needed it. I mean, about everybody I know needs our product, but all they do is whine about how they feel...they won't even try it.
So that means they're not right after all...even though they need it, 'cuz they're not ready to make a change. Not yet, anyway. Hmmm. Later list, here I come.

Think reading readiness for children. The teacher's job is to expose all the children. Some will go faster than others, no matter how much exposure they receive. When they're ready, they magically 'get it'.
People are in different stages of readiness...for everything in their lives.
Ohh. So that's why banging on 'em doesn't work...bummer.
Your Mission: Expose expose expose, without pressure to them or yourself. When they're ready to make a change, the dance begins...
So, save ourselves for the right ones, huh?
Well, if we want to go fast, that's all.

So uhh, think this means we have to learn all of the ROMs so we each can lead all the teams?
Gol, I hope not! That'd take forever! I'm gonna pick my 3-5, and help set up and run those teams, if I get good at it...
Well my upline told me my new people are supposed to do exactly what I do, so they can 'duplicate' me. What if they wanna do something else? Shouldn't I make 'em do what I do?
Offer new babies a picnic table of approaches. You've got the book now, right? Let them all know from day one that there're lots of ways to reach out and build their team.
Takes the scarey right out of it...
Boy, that's for sure! Remember May?
Then put them together with people doing those things so they're never alone during the reaching out process. Do the 3-5 that you love yourself, and help set up and do those teams. That's the system.
We could do that.
Hmm, picnic table. Sounds good, I'm hungry.

All this team stuff--it's almost like at church...people who believe the same things.
Why do you think they have a meeting every week?
To sell themselves all over again?
Yeah, and tell stories about cool things that happened to them during the week.
And they band together and do other group stuff, like choir, Bible study, softball, volleyball, and cookouts.
Like how about study groups for the ros and cons of the comp plan, or one to review the product benefits and price breaks?
An' how about using them for rehearsals for the ROM's we wanna try?
Or discussing people's goals and obstacles in the way of their success?
Yeah! During the week while DFLs are going out, say. That's how we could spend those hours we've committed to the business.
Maybe at somebody's house or over coffee or lunch somewhere...and new people can come too, with their company binders.
Yeah! And we could do group conference calls for our long distance teammates.

Remember what Jesus said about teams?
Go 2 by 2 or more, town to town, and tell the story-
TEAM
-the story about how they themselves came to believe. And doing new things, and the benefits they got from that. And the cool things they saw happen to other people, too.
So their goal was to get other people to join the program so that they could get those benefits too, right?
And they'd tell others, just like we are, right? So it'd get bigger and bigger...
That's right. And then, what did he tell them to do if the people there still didn't get the big picture- -after having spent reasonable time showing them the program?
I know-he said LEAVE...and make sure you knock the dust off your sandals so you don't catch their kooties...right?
Ha ha ha ha!!!
Why do you think he said that, hmmm?

Because he wanted to be sure his guys didn't catch whatever those guys had. And maybe come down with it, too.
Yeah, that's why they stuck together...so they could help each other keep the faith when it got hard an' all...and make sure nobody caught anybody's anything.
Think the stick-together strategy worked?
I guess!! Jesus only had 12, and now look! A quarter of the world's population is in his group!
Uh, I read that somewhere.

How do I decide what to do each day with my time?
Of all the things I could be doing, what will move my business ahead the most?
Draw up a list of up to 6 things. Then prioritize in order of decreasing importance. Do the first thing first. Nothing else. Till #1 is done.
Nothing else? So, if I see dirty socks on the floor, I don't have to pick them up? If I pass by the kitchen, and see a mess, I shouldn't clean it up, right? Would that be ok?
You mean, during the time you've set aside to build your business?
Well, I'm just so used to picking up all the time, and between my walk from my phone to the bathroom, I see a million things that need doing. So I start, and before I know it, an hour's gone by. And then the kids come home from school.
Well, time for the big decision.
Oh no. Not again--what big decision?

Do you want to keep on picking up socks and cleaning rooms for the next 10 years? Or build a business so you might have other options?
She means, like, then you could hire somebody to do that stuff sometimes, right?
Remember what Emerson said: Do the thing; get the power. So what're you doing?
Ok. That means, whatever we do lots, we get that power, right?
Well, I guess that means you're getting sock power.
I don't want sock power...
Wonder how my family would take that at home? I've always done those things as a mom.
Y'know, that's what I thought, too. But I also had this little voice calling out all the time.
Is this all there is? Me want more!!
Alright! Alright already!

So here's what I did.
I made up my mind to do the business. Partly so I could free myself from the yucky things that I did not want to be doing when I'm 65.
I have other plans- So-
I sat the whole family down, told them what I wanted to do and how it would benefit everyone, including me.
What do you want more? A chance to travel and go to neat places? Go on more weekend outings? Maybe buy a cooler car? Top of the line bicycles instead of hand me downs? All the cool CDs and games? Disneyland? Maybe Nordstrom once in a while instead of WalMart for everything?
Yeah! We're ready! We wannit!
OR I keep picking up your socks, make your beds and keep the place clean, make snacks and meals every night. And then, things stay the way they are right now.
'Oh.'

So, which do you want?
To get different, we gotta do different.
WHY can't we have all the good stuff now?
So 'think different' is not enough, huh?
Afraid not. We've got to actually DO different. Sorry. So, what's it gonna be? Do you want to make a change, or stay the way we are?
I don't wanna stay the way we are, do you?
Yeah! What if it takes off?
Even a little...
I guess we could do some of that stuff ourselves...
Yeah. I can make sandwiches.
Maybe I'll do that business with her when I'm 18-hmmm. Cool.

So now, they do those things themselves or they don't get done. It was a family decision. No guilt.
24-hours/day is all anyone has ever had.
This realization can be mind altering when you think of any of the cool people who have been here or are here right now-- John Rockefeller, Madonna, Spielberg, Oprah, Billy Graham, Bill Gates, Jerry Seinfield, Abraham Lincoln, the Wright brothers, Thomas Edison, Andrew Carnegie... What an impact they had-using the same 24 hours we get.
Don'tcha just hate it sometimes?
-to have to acknowledge how much they did with the same time that the man upstairs gave EVERYBODY? All those people started with no money-and just the usual contacts.
So how did they get so much further than we have?
It's how they spend their time. That same 24 hours we all have. And, how they have spent it for several years or more. None of them made it overnight. They did the thing they do until they made it. Attracting others to their cause along the way which started the wave.
Ahhhhh.

I set my goal for 10 years. 10 years to be a millionaire. That's my major definite purpose. And I've done almost four years already. 7 to go!
10 years! Wow! Killer major definite purpose!
Well, I gave up an 80 hour a week sales management job. I was making $80k a year at it, but I hated it and it was killing me.
The first year and a half, I didn't make more than $30k altogether. I went through three companies, before I found Market America 2 1/2 years ago. My check's gone from $300 to 5 figures a month, finally!
So how are you planning to get to a million a year from there?
Well, where else could I even hope to be making that kind of money in 10 years? I'm gonna be 10 years older anyway. I may as well do something where there's at least a chance of obscene income. If you believe it, you can achieve it. Why not?
Yeah. So how close are you?
My plan is to develop 10 people, who want it like I do, to make their dream income. Then mine's free. One of them is my own husband! All I have to do is stay with it and with them. Plus, I'm getting better everyday I do it. Pretty soon, I'll be awesome! Cool, huh?
Jackie Blasko
Independent rep
Market America

Yeah, well, I'm not gonna let anything interrupt me anymore while I'm practicing 'my thing' from now on.
Yup. My thing has just moved to the top of the pecking order. Otherwise, how can I ever get really good at it?
Is it worth it to you to focus like Madonna or Spielberg or Billy Graham? So you have a chance to get REALLY GOOD at that thing you want to do? That is the question. Remember, only 24 hours...
But what if I want more time, even?
Sleep less. Mary Kay says she did that so she could fit in the new stuff she added to her responsibilities when she started her company.
Boy that's easier said than done. I've tried that and it's been easier for me to turn over...
Get a buddy, who wants change as much as you do, and who will get up early or stay up late with you. Call or meet each other everyday to help keep each other on track.
Yeah, just like the Chicago 6 did every week.
How do you think people keep it together in the beginning? When nobody has any money or guarantee that they'll succeed? Hmmm?

OK, OK so, how do we do this list of 6 things? There's so much 'stuff' to do all the time...
Let's sit down together, make our list, and go through and eliminate things we can put on a later list...
What, of all the things I could be doing today, will move my business ahead the most?
List them and prioritize them in order of decreasing importance. Six is a good number.
6
And then?
Fixate on #1 until you have exhausted everything you can do on it.
Do not pass GO until you've done #1. Then do #2, etc., all the way to the end.
Start each day with your BIG SIX and add more as you scratch off those that are completed. Never more than 6.
6!

Boy we better be careful what we put and how we rank stuff.
Yeah, since we can't go past #1 until it's done-
Let's do these together. Talking about it will help make the choices more clear.
The BIG SIX--hmmm.
Well, one of them has definitely gotta be reaching out, right?
Café
Learning those leading questions is gonna be high on my list.
So if we do all this stuff and prioritize our time, how long should we figure it's gonna take to make it?
Say you're ready to start with a commitment of equal to 3 years FT. Figure 220 working days/year @ 8 hours/day.
Ok. That's 1760 hrs/year. Times 3 years, =5280 hours.
If your success means being ready to commit 5280 hours, you decide how many focussed hours per day you will do. Then you can predict how long it'll take to get a good start. Yes?
Well, uh, I heard this guy Ray Gebauer made a million in a year after only 3 years! 3 years after joining Mannatech he was there!
Three years is good.

Uh, well, actually, uh, I had been doing network marketing for uh, 19 years before that...
Yeah-always part time, and often full time.
!!???!!??
So, you got big people you knew after all those years of doing it?
Actually, uh, one guy I got is 25% of my business-because what's under him is under me. That's the system of network marketing, right? But uh,
How much did you make those 1st 19 years?
I never made more than $1k/month during any of that time.
Ohhhh.
50% of my income, more than half, actually, is from someone I didn't know before-he was brought in by someone else I didn't know before either...thank heavens under me.
I thank God every day.
Ray Gebauer
Top Earner
Independent rep
Mannatech Inc

So is it worth it?
What else could you be doing, that in 19 years, could get you anything like Mr. G's income and lifestyle?
Well, it sure beats sock power--
Yeah. Been there, done that. I want this...I'll have it. Even if it takes 19 years.
How about these guys making 5 figures in their first month? And after a year they're making gangster money?
I'm there. I was makin' five figures in my SECOND MONTH in my company. I like going fast. Why wait? Plus, I can brag on it for the rest of my career.
Mike Dimuccio
Top Earner
Independent rep
Nikken
So, uh, what were you doing before Nikken?
I had just come off another company. We did water and air filtration.
How long were you with them?
13 months. Totally full time, too. I busted my a--
How much did you earn during that time?
Well, uhh, uhh, $1-3k per month. Closer to $1k most of the time, actually. Made car payments that first year. My wife started gettin' pukey. But I had met people in that deal who make 6 figures a month, so I KNEW it could be done...

OK. So, how many people does it take to make most of your money now?
Well I sponsored 65 people right off. Half in month one. Obsessed, I was. I really prospected 10 or 12 people hard, that I knew had been successful before...5 or 6 had previous experience in the business.
So, how many?
OK. I've got one terrific guy who's responsible for over 50% of my income. He's been major successful. 3-4 others do the rest.
What happened to the other people you brought in?
They flaked, pretty much. That's why I like going fast. The pain is quick and the gain immediate...And now, six years later I'm makin' 6 figures a month.
EXIT
My wife loves it...me too...I love my company, my team, everything...
'Do you want it or don't you?' That's what I'm gonna ask all of 'em before I sign 'em up.
Me too. And then, I'm gonna go: 'So, are you willing to do what it takes?'
Yeah! 'Are you smart enough to know it takes a while? Or, d'you want to sit down by the side of the road and whine right away an' let the ankle biters getcha?'

I have this really great prospect, with lots of contacts. I just can't get her to see the big picture and the benefits of the business. What can I do to MAKE her see it? She'd be SO good! What do I do?
DUHHHH!!!!!
Where has this guy been? D'he just walk in or what?
Picture this: You get a call... somebody you know wants to come over and tell you about a possible business venture--something they sound very excited about-
KNOCK KNOCK
Listen, our business is just incredible. Many of us make major money. And if we get a team of us practicing the business out of a single complex, we make a % on all those we get in with us. There's room for a few more bright, ambitious people. You're bright and ambitious, aren't you?
Sounds interesting. So uh, what's the business?
Well, actually, I'm talking about the business I'm in. Did you know that brain surgeons can make well over 6, and sometimes 7 figures a year? And much more when we have a team and earn percentages on other brain surgeons, as well. You know, running clinics for brain surgery.
Brain surgeon? You want me to be a brain surgeon? I don't have any background, never even thought about it...
Well, do you want to make a change or stay the way you are?
Well, I want to make a change, but I don't know if brain surgery is what I want to be doing. I'm sure you'll find someone, but I don't think it's for me.

Look, why don't you meet a few of us? You'll see that maybe it is something you could do. With the right training and attitude, ANYONE can be a brain surgeon.
???! !!## @**? ??
Why don't you come to one of our meetings-then you could really see the big picture--I'm sure you'd change your mind--
What do you think? How does that make you feel? You want the guy to come calling again next week? Think you'll get the big picture then?
Well, I never thought of it like that--maybe I'll just try some other people instead.
Plus that doctor guy didn't even know the leading questions. He just starting talking non-stop!
Mission: find the right ones.
Wow! Cool. I never heard about that stuff before!!

I know this sounds stupid, but what if somebody asks me something, and I don't know the answer?
Gee, I'm not programmed that far, but I'll let you know as soon as I find out, ok? So ask me something else...
What do I do if I'm having a bad day and can't get it up?
Do something else already. It's ok. Work out, do self study, contemplate an affair, read something uplifting or entertaining, go to a movie. Until you feel you can be around people without being a drag on them. (Unless it's your shrink, who gets paid to listen to you while you're temporarily overcome by your inner pukey.)
How can I overcome my fear of approaching people?
Don't. Do things that make 'em come to you. Then just zip through the leading questions. Next?
How can I stop blathering to people? I know I shouldn't, but I can't help myself - I'm just so excited...and I think if I can just tell them everything I know, maybe they'll get excited too!!
Keep the LEADING QUESTIONS smack in front of you. And do NO CALLS ALONE. Nearly everybody in sales has to overcome the urge to blather when someone shows an interest. Doing calls with your upline/downline/sidelines helps you be conscious of it, feel accountable and get over it.

How do you get somebody to try the product?
Your own story (results) is best. Second best: stories of others, especially people you are close to where you have the inside scoop and credibility to talk about it.
What if they still won't try it?
Say no first! Or if you're feeling playful, and have the time, like the person, AND YOU've had results, how about:
...before X, I had lots of little aches a pains. Since X, they've pretty much gone. Plus, I got my old energy back, and you know how that can be good for lots of things, right?
Well, I don't know...hmmm
What if it works for you the way it did for me? What if you love it madly? Then would you want to take it or not? Would it be worth it if it DID get rid of some of that stuff you were telling me about?
Uhhh---
Whadda ya, reading the paper or something? Look, do you really wanna fix this thing or stay the way you are?
Lissen, it's up you you...you're the one with the problem, not me. Mine's gone. HA ha ha. You wanna see if it works for you or not? Well, I gotta go---if you ever wanna try something that might fix your thingie, give me a call, ok?
Uhhh---

What about sending information packages? It can get expensive just sending them out willy nilly--if you're on the phone with someone, how do you decide whether to send stuff or not?
What if you tried this-
Ok. Here's the deal. I'll send you the info package, if you promise you'll review it within 24 hours of the time you receive it. Then, we can decide if there's a match or not/if you should pursue it or not/if you should try the product or not. Deal?
Well what if they say they can't?
So then, when should I send it so you could review it within 24 hours of the time you get it? So we can see if there's a match or not--you know, between what you might be lookin' for and what we've got...We'll save a tree till you're ready, right?
'That was me!! That's gonna be me!!
What's the fastest way to make $ in this?
'Today-money' can be had every day of the week by selling the product retail to anyone who might benefit from it. Building teams takes longer. Of course they add to your income as they all sell and you earn the percentages.
What about flakey, do nothing downline?
Oie wey! Give them the goodby message. You'll have to give it to them or leave it on their message service. Then, get a new downline...
Goodbye Message
Hey, you know Joe, it's been great leaving you these messages, but I get the feeling this just isn't the right time for you to being doing this business with us... but listen, no hard feelings. I don't want to keep buggin' you about this so, I'm not going to call you any more. You give me a call when you're ready to make that change we talked about.
I'll be right here! Bye!

What if I can't get some people to follow scripts?
Practice doing scripts together BEFORE doing real calls. During practice, there's always someone who, as soon as they pick up the phone to practice a script, rolls up their eyes and spouts forth all kinds of stuff, on and on. And their script is right there in front of them! Great for laughs.
I'm embarrassed to ask this, but I feel really stupid having to go to motivational things to get turned on all the time. Don't get me wrong, I LOVE it once I'm there. But I mean, I KNOW lots of these things already! I just can't seem to make myself do what I know. Is it just me?
Keeping oneself motivated is much like keeping one's stomach happy. After a big meal, who doesn't feel they could go for a week before eating anything again? And yet the next day, hunger pangs are back. This is the same. After a big fix like this, who feels they'll ever need one again? And yet the next day, pukey pangs may be back. So go ahead and give your motivation a fix. A movie, a nap, a funny book or show, a call to a teammate, or, even, The Truth...
What are your pet peeves?
Well, one's gotta be people in high places who act all pukey about 'how to's' they don't happen to like. And these same people, WHO THEMSELVES HAVE NO EXPERIENCE--HAVE NEVER DONE NETWORKING BEFORE, here they are influencing new babies about HOW it should or shouldn't be done. And of course, mostly they just puke on things they know nothing about.
The same. Except they're influencing YOU AND YOUR NEW BABIES--discouraging folks from trying things that might very well work...
They sound like the pukey types we get...
"Blessed are they who have nothing to say and cannot be persuaded to say it."
James Russell Lowell

Napoleon Hill, in his 20+ year full time study of success and failure in life, pointed out that:
"It is characteristic of people who have but a smattering...of knowledge to try to give the impression that they have much knowledge."
What if the big talkers read this?
Uh, they might get mad...So, uh, what other pet peeve?
Corporate and industry leaders continuing to perpetuate the myth, especially among new babies, that: ANYone can do this. Piece of cake. Just talk talk talk to everyone you know and you'll get rich, rich, rich.
Right. So why don't they, then? Why's there a 95% drop out rate if it's such a piece of cake?
Boy, those people might not wanna hear that.
Have they read the #1 book on all their own recommended reading lists? THINK and GROW RICH?
Mr. Hill says that "The majority of people who fail to accumulate money sufficient for their needs, are...easily influenced by the opinions of others..."
Zōp

And, what kinds of opinions do you think the 'majority of people' must be getting? Good advice or not so good? If they end up failing because they were influenced by it?
Well, not good, a' course. Otherwise they wouldn't have failed, right?
And who do you think they're getting it from? Hmmm???
"Close friends and relatives... often handicap one through 'opinions' and...ridicule...meant to be humorous. Thousands of men and women carry inferiority complexes with them all through life, because some well-meaning but ignorant person destroyed their confidence through 'opinions' or ridicule."
Think and Grow Rich p. 140-141
Dis is why we're learning all those other ROMs, right?
An' we can also do Dear Friend Letters, right? So we don't just skip over 'em. The right ones can come to us.
Now that you know this about friends, family and neighbors, your babies can be prepared - by you.
It's ok to avoid direct hits on ff&n until your new babies have had the results and experience to withstand any possible pukey response.
So they have a chance to survive the process long enough to find the ones for whom it's the right thing to be doing.

You know how they always say, 'know thyself' and 'to thine own self be true', right?
Cruise through the leading questions now, and tell it like it is. What attracted YOU? That's your 'got to' - the 'know thyself' part. Then, do the knock 'em off the fence questions, and make plans for how you're going to grow your business. Then, choose your ROMs and the teams you want to work with. Get all your babies to do the same.
Only talk about your plans and dreams with like minded people, doers, obsessed people with life force who want you to succeed. They can be people in the business or not. That'll help you be true to yourself and stay the course.
Just for You
-we find the ones for whom it's the right thing to be doing...and sidestep all those uhh, those 95%-ers.
OK, let's hit it...you go first, then help your new babies do the same...ready?
Ready!!!!!

LEADING QUESTIONS

1. What attracted you?

2. Have you ever done this sort of thing before? Like direct sales, or network marketing? Or have you ever owned your own business?

3. Great! What have you done?

4. What, ideally, are you looking for?

5. We're looking for friendly, ambitious and openminded people who can help us recruit and train our sales force. And, when we find one or two key people, we'll help them build a sales force so they'll be getting commissions and overrides on everyone in that team. What do you think about that?

6. Right now we're looking for key people - the ones under whom the rest of the team will be built. In the process of hunting for key people, we always come across part time people as well. And that's great. So let me ask you, how do you see yourself - as a key person, or as more of a part time person?

7. So, do you think you could do something like this? If we showed you how?

8. How would you like to get more information? Do you want to see some printed info, an audio or video? Would you like to meet some of us, so we can check each other out? Or would you like to tune into one of our conference calls so you can see if this is something you can do or not? Great, let's do it. When should I call you next?

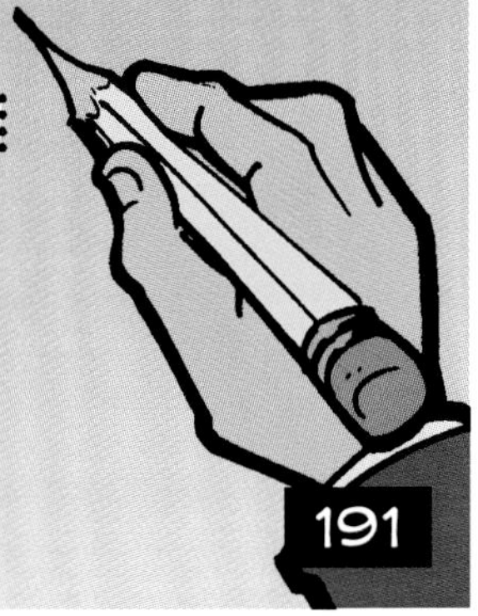

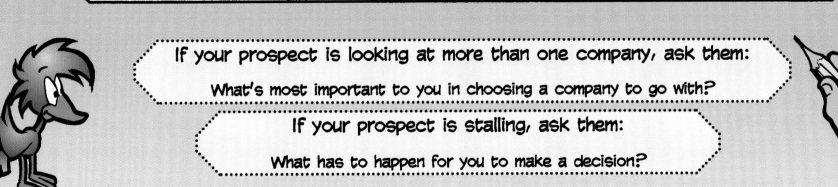

If your prospect is looking at more than one company, ask them:

What's most important to you in choosing a company to go with?

If your prospect is stalling, ask them:

What has to happen for you to make a decision?

KNOCK 'EM OFF THE FENCE

1. OK. Here's what we do: We reach out in lots of ways to find people who'd like to get the same kinds of benefits we get, right? That's what we do to grow our business. You got that part, right?

2. There are lots of ways to reach out to people...whether you know them or not. For example, there are ways that make 'em come to you, and ways where you go first. Ways that cost money and ways that don't. So, you tell me which ones you want to see first, and I'll show you what we do. Then whatever you want to try, you can watch a team that's doing that thing, either in person or over the phone. And after you watch other people doing it, you can try it. Think you could do that?

3. Great, so let me ask you this: How fast do you want to go? Turbo speed, medium, or the leisure track?

4. How much time and money can you commit to building your business in the first six months, whether you make any money or not during that time? Pick a number between say, $50 to $500/mo. or more, you know, for business cards and reaching out. Tell me what you can do, so I can help you get the most bang for your buck and for the time you can commit.

5. When are you ready to get started?

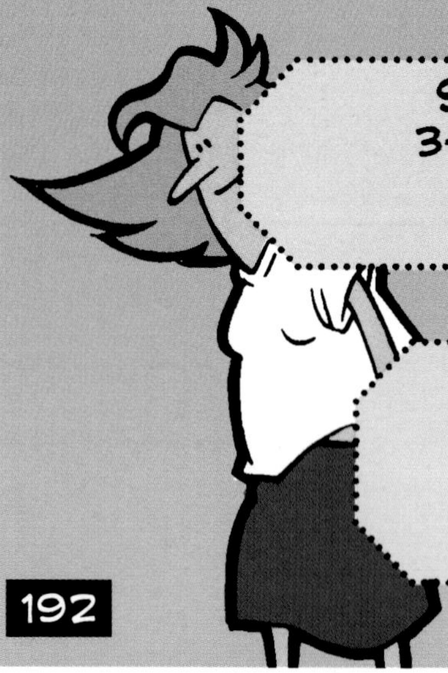

Show your prospect how 'make 'em come to you' really works

3-way them into your 800# voicemail box when it's filled with new leads.
Let them hear for themselves how it's working for you.

Reselling 'em questions

(For those in the heap who are doing nothing)

Remember what you said turned you on about this business when you first signed up?
Is that still true about you?

OK, time to pick your ROMs. Which do you want? Make 'em come to you? Or You go firsts? Or a combo? Use your answers from the knock 'em off the fence script, to determine your time and money options.

People to team up with:

Who?	ROM	When?

Make 'em come to you

Dear friend letter

Local/long distance ads

National co-op ads

Mailing to lists

Card decks

Supercards

Fishbowl

Other:____________________

You go first

Calling Lists

Mall cruising

Street walking

Line surveys (Unemployment office, Kinkos, post office...)

Bump-intos

Presentations to clubs and associations

Trade shows/Street fairs

Business parties

Other:____________________

Here's mine! These're what I'm doing! Which ones did you pick?!?

Want to order more tapes and books from *Ms Stud!*?

Contact Max Out Productions or any of our authorized resellers.

For independent distributors of:

Arbonne, Int'l
Contact: Donna Larson Johnson
800.832.9668 (Wisconsin)

Bodywise Int'l
Contact: Bill Mills
616.828.4809 (Michigan)

Dr. Glen & Dr. Elizabeth Sisk
888.249.1235 (Michigan)

Randy Stralow
309.692.1901 (Illinois)

E'OLA Int'l
Contact: Direct Source
800.494.4659 (Utah)

Excel Communications
Contact: Group Excellence
Marty Huie
800.400.5758 (Washington)

For-Mor Int'l
Contact: David Nelson
303.694.4151 (Colorado)

FreeLife
Contact: Power Players Int'l
David & Coli Butler
909.244.6900 (California)

Matt Silver, MD
410.964.1842 (Maryland)

For independent distributors of:

Kaire Int'l
Contact: Montana Success Center
Greg Mascari
800.848.4481 (Montana)

Mannatech
Contact: Starmaker Services
Ray Gebauer
800.700.1238 (Washington)

Nikken
Contact: Blue Ribbon Video
800.533.2885 (Washington)

Idea Store
800.519.7473 (Washington)

Jerry's Tools
800.404.2433 (Maryland)

John Shorey
603.887.6892 (New Hampshire)

Success Express
800.966.8887 (Washington)

Team Tools Ltd.
800.667.0198 (Oregon)

Nu Skin
Contact: Dave Johnson
702.828.5085 (Nevada)

NSA
Contact: Shining Star Int'l
800.665.1054 (Washington)

For independent distributors of:

Optimal Telecom
Contact: Chris Kent
813.272.1778 (Florida)

Prepaid Legal
Contact: Jan Greene
800.477.7325 Ext.150
(California)

B.J. Kochendorfer
800.307.2898 (California)

Usana
Contact: Direct Source
800.494.4659 (Utah)

Watkins
Contact: GFBS Inc.
800.892.2123 (Delaware)

Rexall Showcase Int'l, I-Link, & Morinda
Contact: Sound Concepts
800.494.4659 (Utah)

And...

Cutting Edge Media
800.561.9297

Opportunity Connection
800.348.4460

PM Marketing
800.864.6371

Upline Magazine
888.875.4631

Special Vendors for conference call services, card decks, name lists and more. Tell them ***Ms. Stud!*** sent you!

Conference Call Svc

Customized Platform Svc

888.888.9962
www.cpstel.com

Teleconferencing
Monthly to unlimited annual plans

Eagle Teleconferencing Svc

800.778.6338

Teleconferencing, voice mail
Up to 60 minute greeting available

Sparks Communications

800.799.8233

Teleconferencing, voice mail
Fax on demand and 800 numbers

Vialog Communications

800.777.1826

Teleconferencing
Help with call planning

Max Out Productions

800.595.1956

Audio tape series

So, You want to be a Networker?
Humorous introduction to what it takes to make it in Networking
The first date

How to Build a Giant Heap
with or without your friends, family or neighbors
Doing it
Finding the right ones for your business

How to be an Awesome Sponsor
and Keep your Heap
Keeping the good ones in

Live Shows

Motivational entertainment for distributor groups and corporate conventions. Wild special effects, music and hands on training

Training calls

Ms. Stud! live on your conference calls
Special Mastermind series for serious builders

Lead Generation

Cutting Edge Media

Bob Schwartz
800.561.9297

Leads, card decks, magazine ads
National co-op ad campaigns
Training calls

Opportunity Connection

Brian Hunt
800.348.4460

Superleads, card decks, ad campaigns
Help with ad & card designs

PM Marketing

Peter Mingils
800.864.6371

Pre-qualified leads
Free training audio with all orders

Venture Direct Worldwide

Geordie Levitan
212.655.5183

Leading broker for all major card decks and magazine advertising

A long time ago, a bright, ambitious man took up occupation as a sower.
Season after season...
Season after season...
So what do you think he should do?
Shoot the little buggers, right?

He believed. He kept on sowing.
Season after season...
What should he do?
Burn those suckers down!
Yeah, blast 'em outta the ground by the roots!

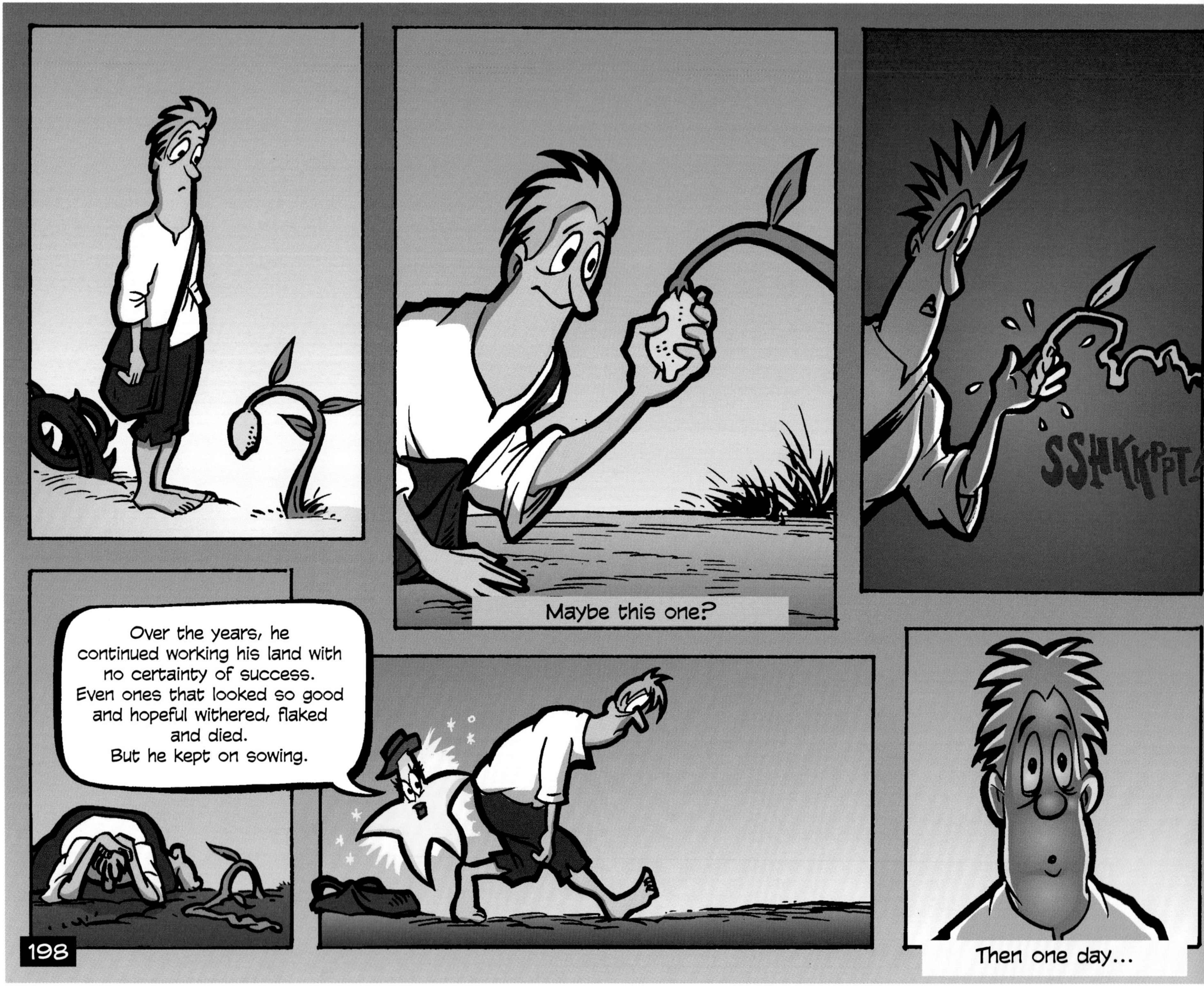

Maybe this one?
SSHKKPPT!
Over the years, he continued working his land with no certainty of success. Even ones that looked so good and hopeful withered, flaked and died. But he kept on sowing.
Then one day...

Some guys get all the breaks.
Yeah, don'tcha hate it? How come I wasn't born lucky like him?
The End

Bibliography

Hill, Napoleon
Think & Grow Rich
New York, NY
Ballantine Books, 1990

Langford, Jerome J.
Galileo, Science and the Church
Ann Arbor, Michigan
University of Michigan Press, 1996

Tzu, Sun
(Trsl. by Thomas Cleary)
The Art of War
Boston, MA
Shambhala Publications, 1988

Redondo, Pietro
(Trsl. by Raymond Rosenthal)
Galileo Heretic
Princeton, New Jersey
Princeton University Press, 1987

Johnson, Caesar
To See a World in a Grain of Sand
Norwalk, CT
C.R. Gibson Company, 1972

Ashe, Mary Kay
You Can Have it All
Rocklin, CA
Prima Publihsing, 1995

Index